Girl with dead bird
Intercultural observations

Girl with dead bird
Intercultural observations

Volkmar Mühleis

LEUVEN UNIVERSITY PRESS

Original title: Mädchen mit totem Vogel. Eine interkulturelle Bildbetrachtung

Authorized translation from the German language edition published by Wilhelm Fink Verlag, München (Germany)
© 2014 German language edition by Wilhelm Fink Verlag, München (Germany)
© 2018 English language edition by Leuven University Press / Presses Universitaires de Louvain / Universitaire Pers Leuven
Minderbroederstraat 4, B-3000 Leuven (België)

All rights reserved. No part of this book may be reproduced, stored in an automated database, or published, in any form or by any means, whether electronic, mechanical, photocopying, recording or otherwise, without the express prior written permission of the publisher.

ISBN 978 94 6270 137 3
D/2018/1869/13
NUR: 651

Translated from the German by John R. J. Eyck

Cover image: *Little girl with dead bird*, South Netherlandish school, ca. 1520. Royal Museums of Fine Arts of Belgium, Brussels.
Photo by J. Geleyns / Ro scan

Design and lay-out: DOGMA

With special thanks to Katlijne Van der Stighelen

Contents

Little girl with dead bird
Art-historical considerations
9-39

Thoughts on life and death (I)
41-59

Intercultural comparisons
61-71

Thoughts on life and death (II)
73-98

Art and anthropology
99-116

Thoughts on life and death (III)
117-140

Notes
143-172

List of illustrations
173

Bibliography
175-179

Little girl with dead bird
Art-historical considerations

A girl gazes out of a picture, past the observer and into the space above. She does not tilt her head, she looks upward with her eyes only. Her entire faces gazes in earnest, with her mouth closed. She is holding a bird in her hands, its head drooping downward, it is dead. The girl is located in front of a wall as dark as night. The background is coloured with shades from her clothing, from her face, shimmering blue, green, almost blackish, then lightening up again, balancing the anonymity, the place. The child – cast in relief before the background, an almost monochromatic background. In front of this unreal background the image appears to be an allegory. This is not any real place. And yet, in this clothing, the girl is a child of her times. What is more, in the art of portraiture during the fifteenth and sixteenth centuries, an almost monochromatic background was customary. Jan van Eyck and Rogier van der Weyden painted in this manner. Yet in this image neither the gravitas of its aura nor its colouring determines the contrast between the figure and the background; the dark of its placelessness appears virtually symbolic. The earnest gaze and the dead bird in hand – they stand out from the dark. Yet because the gaze is not hopeful, not certain, it is in no way clear whether the dark in back does not also cloud the future, the gaze forwards, into the future. And even the light of the figure does not have to be seen as light *upon* it, as a glimmer of hope. In the Flemish tradition, it was customary to understand even the face itself as a source of light, as in the case of Hans Memling, for instance. We might think the girl glows from the inside out. There is no natural light that reaches into the dark background. The reality of her appearance is the relief that is cast, the accentuated image, in front of the dark. We do not know what is standing before her.

*   *   *

The picture *Little girl with dead bird* was probably painted around 1520, as an investigation of its wooden panel revealed. By whose hand is not known. Visitors to the 'Musée Oldmasters Museum' in Brussels only receive simple information on the title given to it by art historians, that it was painted on an oak panel in the 'South Netherlandish tradition', as well as its dimensions: 36.7 × 29.8 cm. In the museum library we come across a few scant sources, essays on the picture and commentaries in catalogues – albeit not any study of its own. Upon closer observation of the portrait, it is striking that the child's right elbow and her right hand are slightly hidden by the frame – that is, the image was not framed to be something autonomous and does not come through as such. What do the restorers have to say in that regard? Which findings are preserved in their dossiers? Over and over again, I found myself standing in front of the picture with visitors, whenever I led them through the museum's collection. For a long time, it hung out in the open; today, it is behind glass. Because the origins and the genre of the picture appear to be unclear – even though it is clearly of outstanding quality – it provides an opportunity like no other picture in the collection to become engaged with a work apart from any information or knowledge, to immerse ourselves in what is simply before our eyes. The picture forces the observer back into 'pre-iconographic' contemplation, the way Erwin Panofsky described the observation that occurs before any iconographic determination of an image based on knowledge from sources, before any iconological interpretation of it.[1] What do we see? A girl, who looks past us, into the distance. She is holding a dead bird in her hands, out in front of her. The little girl is not old, maybe four or five. She is wearing a little white dress – not lily-white but, rather, saturated with colours and shades – with a light blue collar, with an almost rectangular cut to the neckline, without any decoration, only the small rings of her bodice shimmering gold, keeping it stretched tight. The girl is sitting quietly, perhaps at a table, her hands, holding the dead bird, are unusually greyish. What kind of bird is it? Either a house or a field sparrow. Its head droops downwards, two little bones stick up out of tattered feathers on its breast. Perhaps it was killed. By a cat? In a trap? What is the girl's relationship to the bird? She looks concerned but not sad, reticent and yet expectant. She does not know what has happened – her gaze is questioning, as though she needs an answer.

I was once standing with a group of Chinese students in front of the picture. They were on a European tour for the first time, for their European Studies course. It was only then that it occurred to me that the picture contained no symbolism at all that prevented intercultural observation, even though it had been painted in a Catholic Flanders during the rise of the Renaissance and Humanism. A little girl looks into the distance – no matter from where – while holding a dead sparrow in her hands. Life and death are anthropological constants. What distinguish them are the cultural conventions for dealing with each. Might *Little girl with dead bird* be not only an art-historical riddle but also an opening for intercultural observations? This puzzle still prevails, even in the global sense of a museum's day-to-day life.[2] Can answering that question deepen the relationship between art-historical analysis and anthropological interpretation? The latter is elucidated only in the context of intercultural comparison. During the museum tour, I stood with students in front of this picture longer than any other, and asked about their perspectives, impressions, thoughts. It was a starting point, a catalyst for what I wanted to pursue further – precisely because the connection between the history of art and the anthropology of images, as developed by Hans Belting, has until today been a rather exclusionary instead of an effectively complementary relationship.[3]

Could gazing upon *Little girl with dead bird* define this relationship in a new way? This question constitutes the second focal point of the essay, after the first part concentrates on the initially art-historical interpretation of the picture.

Finally, the gaze of the girl holding the bird in her hands, that is, the actual picture itself, constitutes the third focus. Her questioning gaze is still relevant. What would you reply today is the question posed to every observer. What does death mean? And which answer would we give to a child, to ourselves? This third focus unfolds the philosophical dimension of the picture. It, too, relates to anthropological observations, in the intercultural domain. In this way, the interpretation of the picture expands philosophically, taking as its point of departure the relationship of the history of art and the anthropology of images. That is the conceptual linchpin of this essay.

At the same time, this study is an essay because the picture and its subject only allow for a tentative approach. The art-historical riddle will change its shape, expand and deepen, but it will not be (re)solved. As a consequence, rather, we will be able to see what art history in particular is capable of meaning. The subject of life and death offers space for observation and bona fide argumentation, though always in the context of meditation rather than any systematic treatment. And intercultural reflection, the practice of becoming estranged from our own gaze, can only ever succeed in part, remaining unconcluded. These are the limitations of this attempt, yet also its possibilities. I will articulate it in two triad chords, each alternating with the other. The first triad opens the text with an art-historical observation, leading to the intercultural interpretation of the picture and a concluding re-definition of the history of art and the anthropology of images. The second triad discusses one possible response to the questioning gaze of the girl. With that answer, the essay comes to an end.

* * *

In order to do justice to the complexity of the portrait, a commensurate historical analysis is needed, as well as a discussion of the actual experience of its aesthetic. As I indicated, this aesthetic experience no longer operates solely in a Western context. In this first chapter, I would like to concentrate initially on the art-historical presentation of the issues involved, expanding on them subsequently in the chapters on intercultural observations and on the relationship between the history of art and the anthropology of images. At the outset, I already spoke of Panofsky's distinction between a 'pre-iconographic' way of seeing visible phenomena; an iconographic vision that comes through in the work of art against the backdrop of verified sources; and an iconological way of seeing in regard of the space for possibilities of interpretation, in which the sum and substance of a work becomes evident. Max Imdahl later supplemented this distinction with a way of seeing that which was neither unknowing or knowing, but which in its 'pre-iconographic' vision was instead cognition of the formal tensions, through which a work unfolds its, as he wrote, 'aesthetic evidence'.[4] He called this vision 'iconic', one focused strictly on the visible image, as it is with this focus that the mimetic, recognising, analogising, and knowing gaze is first formed. That contrasts with the flashpoints of the image, consolidations of the distinctions adduced in 'formal relations'.[5] What might that mean when gazing at the *Little girl with dead bird*? 'Pre-iconographically' speaking, we have the spontaneous and situational way of seeing. In that vision, the knowledge interest operates by way of concentration, reduction, epoché – as it is called in phenomenology – of certain aspects, in which the way of seeing contrasts, shifts, changes from the 'first glance'. I would like to illustrate this change of view based on the historically varying interpretation of the picture, with respect to those aspects that are still relevant for the experience of its aesthetic. Which sources allow for an iconographic 'epoché'? Additionally, in terms of iconology, what kind of latitude in interpretation results? Further, which network of formal tensions can we talk about in the case of this picture? In order to illustrate the historically varying gaze at the picture as well,

I will treat these questions over the course of that past genealogy, not as strictly separate from one another but, rather, as they appear individually. What kind of history, then, has the portrait *Little girl with dead bird* had?

In 1909, it was shown for the first time publicly in Brussels, in the context of an exhibition for the portrait collection of Count Cavens. It was attributed to Hans Holbein as being a *Portrait of Princess Dorothea of Denmark*. After the count's death thirteen years later, his estate was put up for sale, and the Royal Museums of Fine Arts acquired the unsigned portrait at the second auction in October 1922. It was still considered to be a likeness of the princess, but now by the hand of another Flemish Renaissance painter instead, Jan Gossaert. As heirs of the count, his nephews – Charles de Meulemeester, representing himself and his brother – bore a large portion of the purchase amount for the picture, such that it was declared to be purchased with their support. In the opinion of Joost Vander Auwera – who works today as the senior curator of Old Masters art at the Royal Museums – it may have also had special meaning for the family personally, for their son had died as a young soldier in the First World War.[6] If it is a portrait of the princess, what meaning might be assigned to the dead bird? Soon the picture was seen in general also as an allegory of life and death – by the Dutch poet P.C. Boutens, for instance, who dedicated a poem to the picture in 1942, in the middle of the Second World War. In the original, the two final verses say: 'Want leven is overleven, kind:/Opkomen uit slaap, leed, doodspijn./En pas ervaring bate vindt/Bij 't even flikkrend noodsein...//Doe maar als had je niets gehoord!/En leef naar eigen wijsheid./Daar is niets erger dan kindermoord/Op den langen weg naar de grijsheid.'[7] A translation into English by André Lefevere and Valerie Robillard partly adopts the rhyme scheme: 'For to live, my child, is to survive,/Emerge from sleep, sorrow, pain of death./And only experience does benefit/By life's flickering signals.//Just act as if you did not hear/And live by the light of your own wit./On the long road that brings greyness near,/No crime worse than to kill a child's spirit.'⁸ The translation of 'wijsheid', wisdom, works quite well in 'And live by the light of your own wit'. For the sake of the rhyme, Lefevere and Robillard have interpreted the singular 'kindermoord', infanticide, as being that of a 'child's spirit', which is certainly possible. In this way, multiple ways of reading result: Boutens obviously perceived the gaze of the girl to be uncertain, questioning, and saw the picture allegorically as a question on life and death, which he tried to answer as an observer, as a poet. He turns directly to the little girl, 'kind', 'my child'. What, though, does infanticide mean? Boutens wrote his poem in 1942, as an answer to a child who – just like the little girl in the picture, possibly, at the beginning of the sixteenth century – experiences war, persecution, even 'infanticide'. Might the killed bird be a symbol for a killed child? Might the little girl herself be this child? Or is 'killing' meant metaphorically, like the murder of the questioning spirit of the child, as that spirit also shows in all its directness and openness?

For the heirs of Count Cavens, the portrait may have already been a symbolic souvenir, a memento mori to the death of the child in their own family, during the First World War. Yet would such a way of seeing be plausible for the creation of the portrait as well? The cropped right arm of the girl already raised the question as to whether the picture is an individual piece at all, and whether it can be interpreted as such. Looking at the exhibition of children's portraits in the Low Countries between 1500 and 1700, which included the *Little girl with dead bird* at the Museum of Fine Arts in Antwerp in 2001 (different to the presentation of the show in Haarlem's Frans Hals Museum), Lauran Toorians points out that deceased and/or stillborn children were traditionally also depicted in group portraits of children or families with, for example, a small cross above the head of the child symbolising its death.⁹ We could assume that precisely because of the high infant mortality rate at that time, such a portrayal – despite all grief – was not perceived to be extraordinary or scandalous (all the more so, given that the Christian doctrine of salvation promised 'innocent children' the kingdom of heaven). In that regard, Toorians recalls the 1621 post-mortem portrait for the children of Jacobus Pieterszoon Costerus and Cornelia Jans Coenraadsdochter, put on display from the collection of the art museum in Dordrecht: 'Inscriptions give the names of the children and the number of days and hours each of them lived as well as a line from Psalm 127 on a banderole: *"Lo, children are an heritage of the Lord: and the fruit of the womb is his reward."* Individual portraits of infants and toddlers on their deathbeds occur as well and have lost nothing of the power to move over ages.'[10] Grief and trust in God were not mutually exclusive, and neither was the joint presentation of both. Does this also apply, though, to the *Little girl with dead bird*, a hundred years earlier? The child is not identified, depicted as being dead, or mentioned by name; no symbolic or biblical reference reinforces trust in God; and in concluding even Toorians limits himself to saying, in accordance with the exhibition organisers, that '[i]t is a painting about which virtually nothing can be said with certainty (...).'[11]

After acquiring the picture, it was initially Leo Van Puyvelde, the head curator of the Museums of Fine Arts, who focused on the portrait at length, giving it full technical attention. Summarising his studies in 1948, he wrote in the Brussels arts journal *Les Arts Plastiques*: 'I have spent twenty years next to this painting, a very simple effigy of a child of three years who, with an air of sadness, holds a dead bird in her little hands. I was never able to look at this face without experiencing the very sweet, very sincere emotion that every visitor to the Brussels museums feels when first coming in contact with and stopping before this charming and at the same time profound œuvre.'[12] Is the facial expression *sincère*, as he writes, the picture *charmante*? The facial expression is *collected*, but not certain. The child looks upwards, without speaking. It has no answer for what has happened, for what has changed. The bird is dead. It head lowered, its neck open, we see two bones sticking out. It was killed.

The death appears not only to be fate. The bird did not die a natural death. It was hunted.

The death appears to be an injustice.

As if it belongs to the circle of life?

The girl remains mute. She only looks upwards.

What might Van Puyvelde mean with the designation *charmante*? Certainly not *lovely, delightful, charming*. Shortly afterwards he writes: 'What makes this painting worthwhile is the very illuminated physiognomy of the inner life and the modesty of this feeling of sadness so delicately expressed; it is, above all, the technical means which the artist uses to express his emotion.'[13] In this case, *charmante* could be still best translated as *endearing*. Even for the art historian, the girl is her own source of light. What endears the girl to the observer? For the girl conveys the entire setting. It is about a child, to be sure, and it is about an expression only a child can have – in an adult, distress about the death of a bird would only be experienced as sentimental. At the same time, though, the child has nothing childish to it at all. In the figure of a child its gaze is dead serious – slightly from below, uncertain, inhibited, but nevertheless a direct, open, straight-on gaze.

It is obvious that the painter aspired to this ambivalence. For the execution of the picture denies any sentimentality, as Van Puyvelde adduces. Precisely in this regard lies its timelessness and topicality. It appears to be a timeless allegory of an historical date, valid for the time of any life, *lifetime* ('*Lebenszeit*', in the words of Hans Blumenberg). A picture on life and death. The girl awakens from her childhood existence ('Dasein'), experiences the transitory nature of life, as represented by the bird in her hand. The question *where do I come from, where am I going?* occurs to her for the very first time. What is historical breaks in, into her particular life, having some *intuition* that she is transitory. Even if it is only a bird – children feel affinity with everything that is vital, living; it is only a bird, but did it not fly and sing just as I like to sing and jump? And then the adults will say, it is only an animal. Yet what does that mean to me?

Can we ascribe all that to a child of three, though? Perhaps we ought not do that if, as an allegorical figure, the girl is removed from everything empirical. At the same time, she is not any religious figure, not a girl 'moved by God', the way they were, say, in the courtly romance of medieval literature, like in the German epic poet Hartmann von Aue. She embodies an uncertainty, not an epiphany. She is not innocence personified. Her body seems to be sitting there completely at ease; the position of her arms is nearly enclosed in the vertical rectangle of the picture. Her clean dress, without ornamentation, white, with a light blue border on the neckline, is laced up, tight, even the folds in the sleeves show the tautness of the material. She is in no way removed from the empirical. She herself is part of a history. On her head she is wearing a white bonnet with a light blue border that matches her dress. Is it a gleaming white – the white of a 'bride'? No. It stands out amongst the gradations of the grey tones, shadings. It is an 'earthy' white, not soiled or dirty, just tinted, in the way colours fade. The little girl could be three years old, perhaps even four or five. Later on, would she still be distressed about the death of a bird? Perhaps. Yet the question as to her own particular origins is raised quite early, if the child indeed assumes that she has always already existed, even though her parents tell her that that is not the case, and even though it becomes increasingly evident that there is a pre-history that only her parents know. Into these initial questions comes the death of this bird, awakening anxiety, the question of the *future*. At this moment, the girl has no more than a cluelessness, a lack of intuition, but she experiences that lack as unsettling, no matter how quickly she may again overlook it, or her parents quiet her, or everyday life takes its course.

Which gaze at the portrait does Van Puyvelde additionally offer? In his eyes, the girl appears 'with the distinctness of a sculpted bust'.[14] Both of the arms fall within the right angles of the painting's format and yield the impression of a steady, fixed arrangement. With respect to sculpture of the late fifteenth century, Heinrich Wölfflin had drawn attention to the 'tectonic firmness' of its figures (in the work of Benedetto da Majano, for example).[15] Likewise, this firmness involves a tactile quality, which is conveyed in the picture of the girl moreover by the material of her dress, in its folds, the cut of the seemingly transparent neckline, the taut laces. Van Puyvelde shows how this visual quality, too, is achieved formally through reference to the connections between the light blue shades in the picture: the neckline is framed by the same light blue that defines the colour of the girl's eyes as well as the blue border of her bonnet. In this way, the 'tectonic firmness' is formally emphasised by the rectangular cut to the neckline and at the same time is visually nuanced in its transparent appearance. In terms of its shape, this cut carries the head in terms of form, just as the border of the head covering constitutes its counterpart, also framing the head, out of which the gaze of the girl, again in the same blue shades, speaks to us.

From 1924 to 1937, Max J. Friedländer published his fourteen-volume compendium *Die Altniederländische Malerei* (translated as *Early Netherlandish Painting* [Leiden, 1967-1976]), and Ludwig Burchard, who was in contact with Friedländer, turned to Van Puyvelde with a view to the acquired portrait of the little girl. Thus began the first art-historical elaboration of the portrait, in the initially close exchange between Van Puyvelde and Burchard, in 1931. Thus, for instance, the art historian in Berlin wrote to his colleague in Brussels: 'I briefly showed the photo [of the painting] to Dr. Friedländer. (...) He would very much welcome it, if this likeness, which has always intensely interested him, were cleaned.'[16] Both agreed that the background had been overpainted. Burchard conjectured that 'the shadow on the right side of the head' had been overpainted, by comparing it with a portrait of a girl painted by Juan de Flandes, whom both

Van Puyvelde and Burchard assumed to be the painter of this picture, contrary to its attribution to Jan Gossaert.[17] Their comparison would not prove to be true, but the conjecture concerning overpainting 'on the right side', specifically of the 'head shadow', would later be confirmed and even expanded – by another, different head shadow.

Using a microscope, Van Puyvelde investigates the possibilities for conducting a 'cleaning', for uncovering the complete original. Only a few days afterwards, he answers Burchard: '(...) you have seen, the background was initially a clear green, I think, but I could still not assess if it was verdigris. It is still very visible underneath the frame; this green has been covered by a very opaque brownish colour (...).' The background had initially been more greenish – Burchard could not clarify whether it was verdigris ('vert-de-gris') – and was then covered with brownish-black. From when, though, did the overpainting date? Was it *pentimenti*, original corrections by the artist? Or later adjustments, reworkings, by another hand, during another period? In the French journal *Journal de radiologie et d'électrologie* from 1933, Van Puyvelde published his findings on x-rays of portraits, including the *Little girl with dead bird*. Concerning this painting, he wrote: 'On the child's forehead, there is a greyish colour that I believe is from restoration; perhaps, I said to myself, the x-rays would detect additional repaintings. I x-rayed the painting. On the x-ray, the repainting does not project any shadow. And the x-ray detects a couple of instances. Visual examination reveals that these instances have been made by the same impasto as the rest, and that they are all corrections. They are not repaintings for removing anything; they are repaintings by the artist, who was working slowly and correcting his work himself.'[18] Van Puyvelde therefore assumed that that it was a correction by the artist in the case of these overpaintings 'on the right side' on the 'shadow of the head'. He said nothing in this article as to the brownish-black overpainting of the green layer below. In 1935, Joseph van der Veken succeeded in removing the very dark overpainting, such that under the green layer, another light blue background could be substantiated.[19]

ART-HISTORICAL CONSIDERATIONS 21

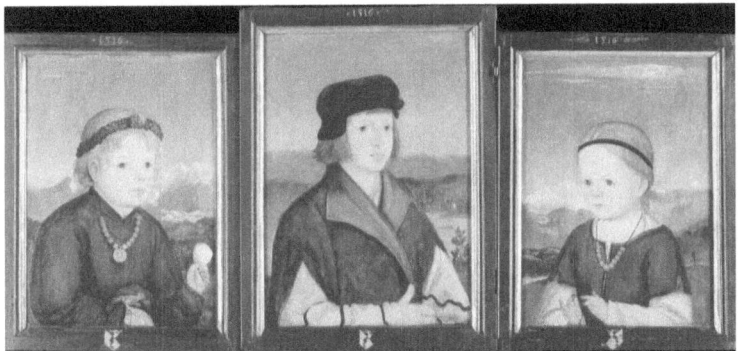

Ill. 1. Master of the *Thennsche Kinderbildnisse* ('Likenesses of the Thenn Children'), *Three Children of Johann Thenn, Master of the Mint*: Likeness of Ruprecht Thenn, lime tree wood, 43 × 34 cm; Likeness of Wolf (?) Thenn, lime tree wood, 46.80 × 36.20 cm; Likeness of Barbara Thenn, lime tree wood, 43.20 × 34.20 cm; Frankfurt, Städel Museum, photo by U. Edelmann

In summarising his studies in 1948, the curator took pains to clarify the painting's authorship. In so doing, he took the following hypotheses as his point of departure: At the beginning of the sixteenth century portraits were made only of royal children ('During this period, only the children of princes benefitted from such an honour.'[20]); for the Southern Netherlands at this time, the painters 'Jacopo de Barbari, Pierre van Coninxloo, Jean van Roome, Bernard van Orley et Jean Vermeyen' are documented at the court of Mechelen[21]; stylistically speaking, however, the picture would be closest to the work of Juan de Flandes; did this painter have the opportunity, then, to paint, the princess at the court of Mechelen at that time, during her childhood years, namely, little Margaret of Austria, the subsequent governor of the Habsburg Netherlands? Even the first assumption does not hold water. In Salzburg, contemporaneous to the *Little girl with dead bird*, the 'Likenesses of the Thenn Children' ('Thennschen Kinderbildnisse') by a similarly undetermined Master were created (Ill. 1). They show the three children of the Master of the Mint, Johann Thenn II. They are neither princes nor princesses,

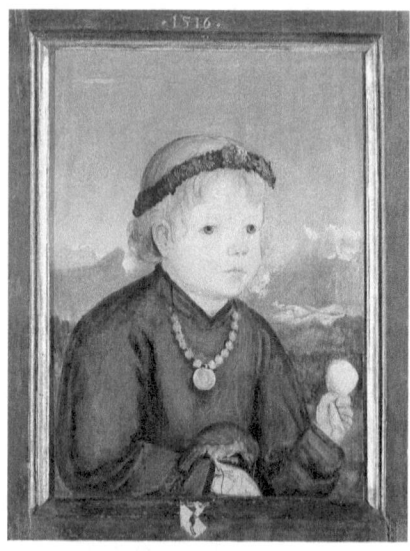

Ill. 2. Master of the *Thennsche Kinderbildnisse*, *Likeness of Ruprecht Thenn*, lime tree wood, 43 × 34 cm, Frankfurt, Städel Museum, photo by U. Edelmann

even if the family is depicted with their coat of arms. Symbols for the children point ahead to their subsequent destinies: So, for instance, the oldest is wearing the garb of a young scholar, the brother has a sparrow on his hand (Ill. 2), and the little sister plays with a cherry between her fingers. Which destiny does the sparrow foretell in this case? That of a hunter. The pictures are found in Frankfurt's Städel Museum, and the text of the museum catalogue notes: 'The four-year-old Ruprecht plays falconer – albeit with a sparrow that sits on his falconer's glove!'[22] The sparrow as a playmate, as the visual representative for the actual destiny, the falcon, the hunt. Can conclusions be drawn from this portrait for the dead sparrow in the girl's hands? She does not have any cherry for getting married at some point. Why, then, this dead sparrow? Is she not to become a playmate, a 'lovemate', herself? Is there any predestination for her, aside from sensuality and eroticism? Or might this direction once again be thinking things too far?

One year following Van Puyvelde's interpretation in *Les Arts Plastiques*, a reply appeared in the same journal from A. Duflou and

J. Van Opstal, in which the additional hypotheses were also convincingly called into question.[23] Both the attribution to Juan de Flandes — I will not go into the specifics of the debate on the authorship, since it has continued to this day, without any substantive result[24] — as well as the identification of the girl as another Margaret of Austria are unlikely. A children's portrait of this princess found in the palace at Versailles notes, in French and Dutch, that it was painted in 1483, when little Margaret was three years and three months old. The style of the portrait shows Gothic traits; any similarity of the princess to the girl in the Brussels picture cannot be determined; moreover, decorative insignia identify her as a royal child; and, last of all, the question remains as to how the *Little girl with dead bird*, which was clearly painted in the Renaissance style after 1500, can show the princess as a small child, whereas from that time forward she was already an adult.

In 1965 and 1966, the painting was x-rayed multiple times, in the Institut Royal du Patrimoine Artistique (IRPA) of the Royal Museums of Art and History in Brussels. The director of the IRPA, R. Sneyers, summed up the findings in two letters to the head curator of the Royal Museums of Fine Arts, Ph. Roberts-Jones. In the first letter, dated 17 December 1965, he notes the following results: There is a shadow in the background that is almost completely hidden; underneath the overpainting, the girl's waist is decorated; her chin was originally longer; the eyes are clearer than we see them today; the size of the figure has been changed; her mouth shows traces of overpainting, and the green background, too, has been heavily painted over.[25] In the second letter, dated 21 March 1966, the entire scope of the picture's historical creation becomes clear: Parts of it were restored before the twentieth century, and it contains corrections even from during its creation in the sixteenth century. How, then, do these parts correspond to the original? For one, the picture today shows signs of wear — in the shadows, on the right hand, to the right of the bodice, on the inside of the right arm. For another, it was restored — on the left nostril, in the area of the upper lip, on the right.

Attempts at touch-ups left behind spots on the neckline and the right shoulder. The background was renewed in the corner below on the right. Above and beyond that, there are early overpaintings or alterations – the iris in the right eye, a shadow in the background under the right shoulder, the shape of the neck and part of the shoulder with respect to the contour for the bluish background, a correction by the painter on the right shoulder. In addition, finally, the question arises as to how the restoration and the painter's own touch-ups correspond to one another. The first, green background consists of two or three layers of verdigris and a drying oil – entirely in the way Van Puyvelde had conjectured – covered by a layer of blue made from sky blue (azure), ochre, white, and oil. Since no evaporation took place on the blue layer, any alteration made shortly after the blue matter dried can be ruled out. It did not mix with the green layers, so that it is not very likely that it belongs to the picture's original execution. No intermediate layer has formed, and the release of pigments on the surface of the blue layer suggests a blue background that was cleaned and then had been overpainted green (the verdigris, which Van Puyvelde conjectured, thus belongs to the very bottom stratum, underneath the blue, before which a 'green stratum' emerged, as Joseph van der Veken discovered after taking off the brownish-black overpainting).[26]

An entire complex of questions accompanies these findings: questions about the practice of painting, the original, the restoration, as well as questions concerning datability, the evolution of the whole piece, yet those regarding purpose, too – why were these interventions taken and how? For starters, we recognise that we are not dealing with the transmission of *one* original but, rather, that the picture today is the result of a specific evolution, with interventions and alterations. In the art market, according to Joost Vander Auwera, such a portrait would not be treated as an original from the sixteenth century, since more than 20% of the picture is restorations. Yet are they only restorations, or are they interventions that alter the picture? Let us have a look at the catalogue of findings

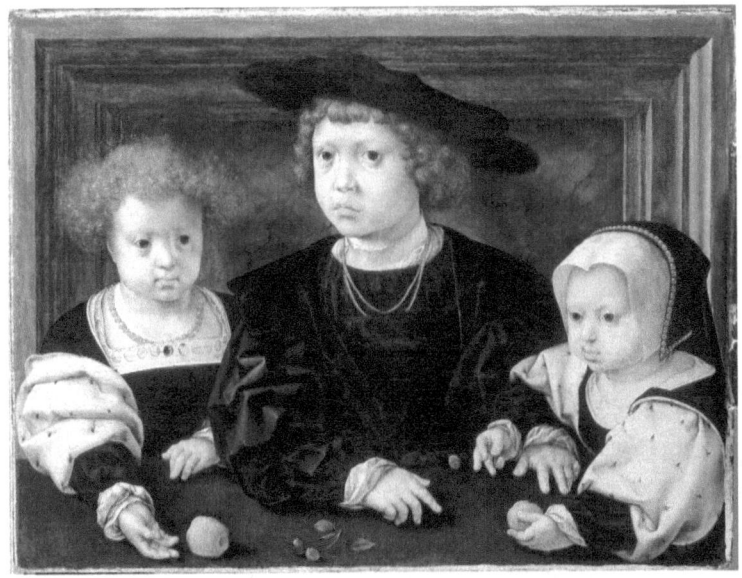

Ill. 3. Jan Gossaert, *The Children of Christian II, King of Denmark*,
oil on oak panel, 34 × 46 cm, 1526, London, Collection of Her Majesty
the Queen of England by permission of the Royal Collection Trust /
© Her Majesty Queen Elizabeth II 2017

from x-raying the picture. 'There is a shadow in the background that is almost completely hidden.' Did the painter overpaint an earlier picture? Part of his own touch-ups also includes overpainting a shadow in the background of the right shoulder. Or was the picture originally not an individual portrait but, rather, one showing several figures, like in the group portraits of children in one painting, for instance, in the likeness of the three children of Christian II of Denmark, which Jan Gossaert painted (Ill. 3)? Is that why the picture is cropped below on the left? 'Under the overpainting, the girl's waist is decorated.' Was the dress initially decorated instead? Was the part by the bird made more unadorned in order to have it appear that much more contrasting in front of a white waist? Does the fact that the chin was longer and the size of the figure altered relate to the corrections the painter made to the proportions of the neck and shoulder portion? Originally, the eyes were clearer, 'plus nets', less blended, more distinct than today. In that regard, the iris in the right eye had already been touched up at an 'earlier time' (being 'surpeint ancien', as the report by R. Sneyers calls it – cf. the original text of the letter in note 25). In the gleam of the eyes, accordingly, the gaze that is so decisive for the picture's suggestive effect has changed, although that change had already been executed in the premodern era. The later restoration concerns the left nostril; in this restoration, shadows and spots remain on the neckline and the right shoulder. Most important, however, is the restoration of the upper lip, on the right, and of the background, just below in the corner on the right. How did the adaptation of that part of the mouth relate to the facial expression? And why was there any restoration in the picture just below to the right? Was it also damaged there? In the overpainted shadow to the right of the child, according to Joost Vander Auwera, there is the shadow of the head of an additional figure, which would have to have been located to the right of the present image, within the framework of a group portrait. Was this group portrait damaged in turn, and only the section of the girl with the bird retained, adapted to the requirements of an individual picture, by making the background match? This would explain the initially black-brown overpainting of the background, which Van der Veken had removed. The stratification of the background constitutes an additional riddle. Does the fact that there was a longer period of time between the strata of the verdigris and the blue layer speak to the idea that the painter was working 'slowly' – as Van Puyvelde thought in the beginning (cf. note 17) – or that both strata come from different times, and that the picture originally had a green background?

The comparison with the likeness of the three children of Christian II of Denmark by Jan Gossaert opens up an additional level, namely, regarding the topoi of general sites for portraying children in the sixteenth century. In their discussion of the portrait, Desmond Shawe-Taylor and Jennifer Scott recall that part of the visual topoi of the era included portraying children earnestly, down to their very gaze.²⁷ Is the earnest gaze of the girl with the dead bird truly owing to the dead bird, the way she appears in the extant picture? In comparison with the children of the Danish king, only his son, John, gazes into the distance in a similarly oblique way. Why, though, does his gaze not appear to be questioning? Because it is surrounded by the entire stately scenography of a portrait of royal children. Gossaert's picture does not call any form of representation into question. The girl's gaze into the distance, however, is only effective as a result of the dead bird – yet as disregarding and looking towards what? This tension creates an opening for uncertainty, enabling interpretational latitude, in a way that the symbolism of aristocratic representativity during the Renaissance did not provide (only later, during the Baroque, would Diego Velázquez carry this courtly representativity into uncertain interpretational space, with his portrait *Las Meninas*²⁸). Would this effect change, if 'John' were isolated and given a dead bird in reworked hands? No. He would look amazed, somewhat chubby-cheeked, but not off into the distance, like the *Little girl with dead bird*. In that regard, the placement of the eyes and the treatment of the pupils and iris are pivotal. The iris was corrected in an 'earlier time' – it is meant to be premodern, whether by the painter himself or by another hand. Even so, between painting the original and reworking it there can be a lot of time that goes by, perhaps a journey, or transporting the picture, accompanied by the same painter, who then has to touch up the damages that his work incurred along the way. In the 'premodern era', Pieter Paul Rubens wrote to Annibale Chieppio, on 24 May 1603, that 'the paintings that I sent and packed as carefully as possible with my own hands (…) showed up in the house of Mr Hannibal Iberti today, rotten and damaged to such an extent that I almost despair of being able to restore them.'²⁹ In that way, touching up the iris could indeed be by the hand of one artist. What remains suspect, though, is the alteration of the green background into a blue one. This change is conceptual, not any slight adaptation of what there is. Might that also be 'by the hand of one artist'? Or the consequence of a fundamental reduction of the motif to an individual image – by analogy with Sneyer's refutation, an 'original execution' of this change – inasmuch as the dark background adapts the image to the conventions of the Flemish art of portraiture during the Renaissance or even intensifies the allegorical dimension of the representation? Might this alteration still be plausible in the Renaissance, or only later?

In 1968, Bob Claessens argued in favour of its plausibility during the Renaissance. In his discussion of the *Little girl with dead bird* for the Brussels art journal *Peinture vivante*, he writes: 'The Renaissance – in inviting the individual to reflect on the problems of earthly life with the acuity that the Middle Ages brought to those of the afterlife, and in putting the emphasis on individualism and human dignity – quite naturally, in painting, put the emphasis on technique and on the art of portraiture. (...) The individual portrait, free from every Christian theme, would soon seduce Van Eyck. (...) we believe the Little girl with dead bird to be a work that also takes place during the initial years of the Renaissance (...). We do not know of any other work, dating from this era, in which the sentiments of the figure portrayed – chagrin, surprise, tears – are displayed in such a way in public (except in religious paintings, of course). This emotion from the painter and his model, as well as the addition of the frail cadaver that the child holds between its hands, turns this panel into a "genre painting", a neglected type in this era. (...) Certainly, the problem of death preoccupied Renaissance painters, yet for the first time in the history of painting, it is a child confronted with the problem, and that gives this painting (...) a resonance particularly dolorous and profound.'[30] Might the commission for the picture have come, for instance, from the circle of South Netherlandish humanists? In 1517, Quentin Matsys painted the portraits of Erasmus of Rotterdam and of the Antwerp scholar and municipal clerk Pieter Gillis. Since Antiquity – the study of which flourished amongst humanist circles – the sparrow in the girl's hand has been traditionally interpreted as a playful, sensual bird that likes to mate. Patrick De Rynck points out that likewise at the beginning of the sixteenth century – when the *Little girl with dead bird* was created – the Dutch scholar Johannes Secundus was writing his 'kiss poems' as imitations of Catullus.[31] Although Secundus' *Liber Basiorum* was only published posthumously in 1541, he had been friends with Erasmus of Rotterdam, on the one hand, and had lived, on the other hand, in the South Netherlandish town of Mechelen since 1528. Already, when looking at the 'Likenesses of the Thenn Children' ('Thennschen Kinderbildnisse'), we wondered whether the dead sparrow could be meant to be a promise, whether this girl within the familial order was predestined not to be a 'lovemate', nor for marriage – but instead, perhaps, fated to a life for the Church? The lively sparrow was part of the store of Renaissance subjects, as the picture of Ruprecht Thenn demonstrated. Yet ought the *dead* sparrow not be seen explicitly against the backdrop of Catullus' love poetry, the way it was received during the Renaissance even in Central Europe in isolated instances?[32] Let us look closely, then, at what this poetry has in common with the dead bird in the hands of a girl, and to what extent it can be related to the Brussels picture.

Any possible relationship between text and image would in no way have to have been purely illustrative, as is shown with the portrayal of the fall of Icarus from the atelier of Brueghel, for instance, adapted freely from the telling of the myth in Ovid's *Metamorphoses*. What Ovid mentions in passing ('some idle shepherd leaning on his crook, / some plowman at his plow') the Brueghels move into the foreground of the composition, while the main event – Icarus' fall – wanders down into the lower right corner of the picture.[33] In the case of Catullus, there is only an indirect relationship between text and image, if that. For the girl in his poetry is Lesbia, his beloved, whom he attempts to console after the death of her beloved sparrow, with the following words: 'Lesbia, let us live only for loving, / and let us value at a single penny / all the loose flap of senile busybodies! / Suns when they set are capable of rising, / but at the setting of our own brief light / night is one sleep from which we never waken. / Give me a thousand kisses, then a hundred, / another thousand next, another hundred,/a thousand without pause and then a hundred/until when we have run up our thousands/we will cry "Bankrupt!" hiding our assets/from ourselves and any who would harm us,/knowing the volume or our trade in kisses.'[34] The fact that we can indeed imagine Lesbia to be a child by today's expectations is shown in images from the eighteenth century. For example, someone who explicitly referred to Catullus' song for Lesbia was Joshua Reynolds. He himself sold one of his portraits under this title in 1786. It shows a girl, dreamily gazing just past the observer – her left arm placed on a cage – as she pets a sparrow on its beak and plays with it (Ill. 4).[35] This girl has not yet reached puberty, yet is clearly older than the girl in the Brussels portrait. A girl of 'primary school age' we might say today, perhaps, whereas the child in the Brussels picture would not be a 'schoolchild' yet – historians estimate her to be, even by her clothing, three or four years old; she might even be five, though certainly not as old as the figure portrayed by Reynolds, by comparing only their hands: rounder, more childlike (stylised) in the Brussels picture – more supple, open, 'languid' in Reynolds. And the slightly flowing dress and the relaxed stance of his *Lesbia* could betray erotic, seductive instances as well, for an adult (even though the child is perhaps only posing as a 'princess'); yet in the Brussels picture, the child's austere dress and her bonnet emphasise the gravitas of both her gaze and her stance.

At this juncture, the comparison with Reynolds opens up additional, surprising perspectives for art-historical observations. Reynolds (1723–1792), that is, similarly portrayed a *Girl with a Dead Bird* in two versions, which clearly make reference to Lesbia's grief for her house or field sparrow (Ills. 5 and 6). Different to *Lesbia*, this girl is not wearing any jewellery, her hair ribbon is unadorned, as is her light-coloured dress. The dead bird is resting in her hands on her lap. In two-thirds profile, she is looking at the ground, into the void, the shadow, from which the cage rises. Which meaning is assigned here to the *cage*, say, as a complementary element?

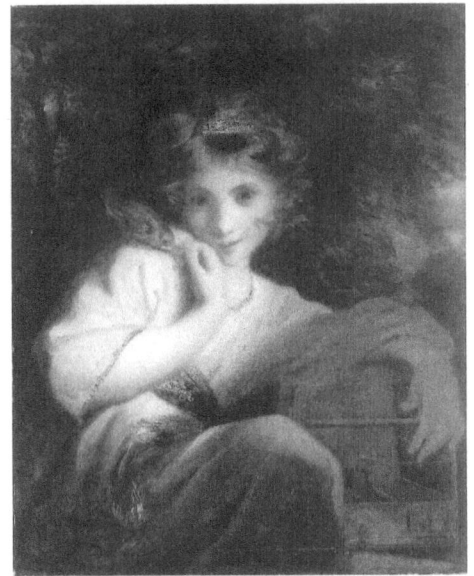

Ill. 4. Joshua Reynolds, *Lesbia*, oil on canvas, undated, 75 × 67.20 cm, London, Tate Gallery

Aside from its foregrounded innocent setting of childlike sorrow, this composition clearly puts the picture – like that of *Lesbia* – into an erotic context. Since modernity – as Eddy De Jongh stated with nuance in his article "Erotica in vogelperspectief" ('Erotica from a bird's-eye view') – the symbolic relationship of bird and cage could be comprehended as part of a sensual spectrum, one which ranged from the metaphor of sensual love to the indication of loss of virginity to the allusion to male and female genitalia.[36] In the first case, the *locked* cage would be an image of those lost in love, in the shape of a bird; in the second instance, the cage would stand for the female sex, and an *empty, open* cage for the loss of her virginity; in the third case, the cage and the bird would correspond, respectively, to the female and male genitalia. In the case of Reynolds' portrayal, only the second way of reading comes into question. The cage is empty, and the bird lies dead in the girl's *lap*. She thus laments the loss of a playmate, a bird, in the foreground, while in the background the picture can be seen as the loss of her sexual innocence.

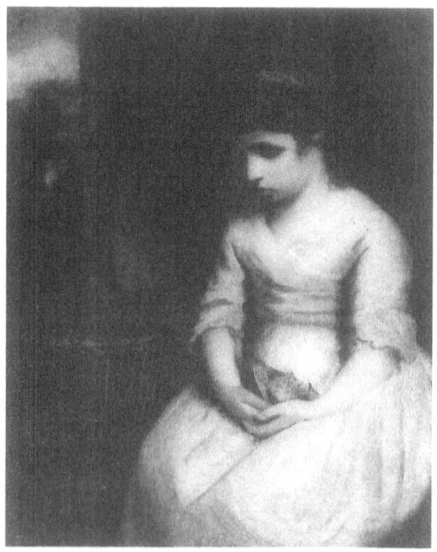

Ill. 5. Joshua Reynolds, *Girl with a Dead Bird*, oil on canvas, undated, 73.70 × 61 cm, private collection (cat. no. 2083)

What is additionally astounding is that the designation *The Little girl with the dead bird* has become established amongst art historians both for this type of portrayal – a girl grieving at the loss of a bird by its cage – as well as for the portrayal in Brussels *without* any cage. The difference is multi-layered: As De Jongh demonstrates, the symbolism of bird, cage, and girl has been well known in an erotic way since Hieronymus Bosch – in his œuvre, birds are repeatedly symbols for obscenity (in the *Garden of earthly delights*, for instance), and Bosch utilises the birdcage as the customary sign at that time for a bordello. It was only after the Baroque, with the Sentimentalist stories of the eighteenth century, that artists like Reynolds or Jean-Baptiste Greuze (Ill. 7) connect the symbolism in question with the image of a *dead* bird. Before then, the *open* cage already meant lost innocence. Now, however, the emotionality of the picture has been heightened, in that the girls concerned do not just gaze after a bird that escaped (as, say, in Willem van Mieris' portrayal[37]). Instead, the bird itself is dead, and neither Reynolds nor Greuze shows any further observation or contemplation by the girls but, rather, the grief of the girls with their heads lowered.[38]

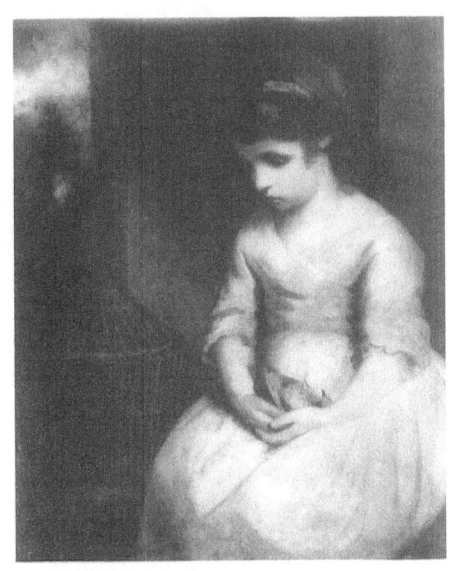

Ill. 6. Joshua Reynolds, *Girl with a Dead Bird*, oil on canvas, undated, 76.20 × 63.50 cm, private collection (cat. no. 2084)

Yet the picture in Brussels shows no cage, that is, no symbol of female sexuality, much less purported corruptibility. The example from Reynolds shows that, during the eighteenth century, the limit for that sexuality was still under the age of puberty – as was the case for corruptibility even in a seventeenth-century picture by Gerard Dou, *Meisje met muizeval* ('Girl with mousetrap'), which De Jongh discusses very vividly.[39] In any case, this limit seems to have been reached in the young age of the little girl in Brussels. With the pictures by Reynolds and Greuze, it becomes evident that there is a genre of *Little girl with dead bird* that has unfolded historically.[40] It is, however, an erotic one, whereas in the Brussels portrait the threshold of the erotic is circumvented, as a result of the young age of the little girl. Thus, when Bob Claessens poses the question as to genre in view of the Brussels picture, he is right – if in fact it was painted as an allegory for the humanists during the Renaissance – that the image has to do with the singular, initial instance of a genre, specifically the painterly reinterpretation of Catullus' verses into an allegory of life and death, in the portrayal of a little with a dead bird, a field or house sparrow.

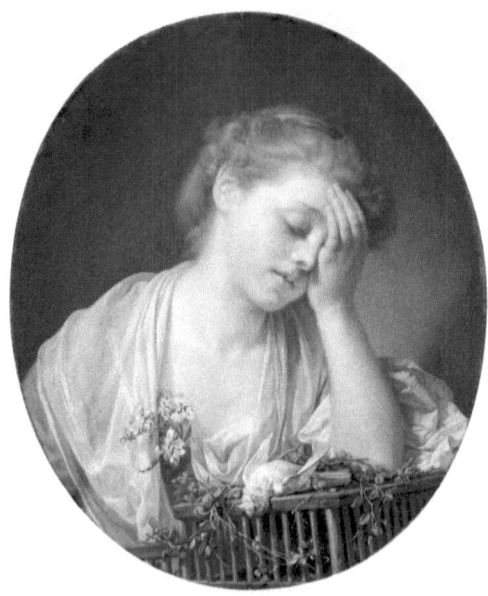

Ill. 7. Jean-Baptiste Greuze, *A Girl with a Dead Canary*, oil on canvas, 1765, 53.30 × 46.00 cm, NG 435, National Galleries of Scotland, bequest of Lady Murray of Henderland 1861

In addition, however, evidence is needed from the verses of Catullus as well. In this regard, there is the poem "Lugete, o Veneres Cupidinesque" ('Cry out lamenting, Venuses and Cupids').[41] The little girl in the Brussels portrait is not Catullus' Lesbia. The poem, in which the grief at the death of the bird is extolled, provides only one line that could have served as inspiration for any representation in the spirit of the portrait in question. That line says about the sparrow: 'It now flits off on its way, goes, gloom-laden / down to where— word is—there is no returning.'[42] It is the way into the 'damned shades of Orcus that devour / all mortal loveliness', as it goes on to say. Even so, Christian trust in God still occurred on the other side of Ancient Rome, during the first half of the final pre-Christian century in which Catullus lived. The *Little girl with dead bird* is a picture on death, apart from Christian symbolism, in the tension between looking ahead and looking deeper, but at what? To the observer it signifies uncertainty like no other picture of this era suggests, as far as I know. Does that come from the reworkings and restoration? The reworkings themselves are in part from an 'earlier time'; the restoration might also derive from the nineteenth century, as part of a 'Romanticisation' of the portrait, as will be discussed below. The questions of the overall effect, though, can only be the following: The figure as such was conceived with the dead bird. The background was initially greenish instead of dark. One of the shadows in that background was painted over – the shadow of another figure? Was it part of a group picture? The eyes were initially more distinct; the iris in the right eye was reworked at an 'earlier time'; the upper lip was restored on the right. The dead bird is original; the very definitive gaze from an 'earlier time', although less distinct, whereby the pupils are not designated as either reworked or restored. The picture's effect today is doubtless different to that in the sixteenth century. A greenish background would remove the drama from the image; and with the shadow of another figure, it could have been fit into a group portrait. Lacking any art-historical equivalents, the motif of the little girl with the dead bird would still have appeared to be singular. Perhaps it would have gained less symbolically loaded significance in an ensemble, in contrast to other representations. On the other hand, the motif itself does not suffer from its possible fragmentation, or from the darkening of the background; on the contrary, the motif gains a kind of force that reaches into the present, an energy that does not even contradict the conventions of the Renaissance – the dark background of a portrait was commonplace, after all – since Jan van Eyck and Rogier van der Weyden. For which possible fragments from the sixteenth century can that claim be made?

Yet we cannot refrain from designating the association of the Brussels image with Catullus to be extremely fragile. Namely, in the same, and only, poem that comes in question as a source, the poet in closing describes the girl's eyes as 'reddening, ruining her eyes from sorrow'. It would not be any argument against this association, if the eyes in the picture did not correspond to the text by degrees.[43] Yet what if they do not do so at all? Contrary to this emotion, the only thing we find expressed in the picture is the topos of the child's seriousness, together with the representation of a dead sparrow in her hands. In this regard, the reference to Catullus is significant, because it represents until now the only demonstrable, possible source indicated for the picture, for the iconographic combination of a dead sparrow with a girl. The fact that this girl is not Lesbia attests to distance of the image from the text. It could have only served as inspiration for transferring its impulse into a new, different sort of coherence, dispensing with the erotic identification with Lesbia in favour of a stronger focus on the opposition of life and death in general, as illustrated in two lives coming to a head, the child's life with all her possible future and the life of the dead bird, whose comparatively short lifespan has already been cut short. In this regard, furthermore, this reinterpretation of Catullus in turn makes an appeal to him in favour of a later, faithful interpretation quite possible. In this way, the *Little girl with dead bird* in Brussels could be related to the later erotic genre of the same name. Given this reading, the Brussels picture would have ushered the motif from Catullus into painting, apart from any erotic interest, in favour of an individual, humanistic view on life and death, in the form of a concentrated allegory. Once introduced, however, it can be moved back into its 'proper' place and handed down as an erotic subject, true to Catullus once again. In doing so, the possible 'reinterpretation' would have remained singular; more indebted to the source and more risqué, this variation would have been continued, not seeing death as such, in contrast to life but, rather, casting it erotically.

In 1994 the *Little girl with dead bird* was examined one last time, comprehensively, without any frame, in ultraviolet light, under infrared radiation as well as an electron microscope – by the Munich art historian Matthias Weniger, no less – with a view to any possible identifiability of the artist.[44] In summarising his analysis, Weniger, too, distinguishes the portrait's original features from reworkings afterwards. Doing so, he writes: 'The sparrow painted so very masterfully belongs to what existed earlier (…). The topic, as related to a genre, was introduced at the latest over the course of the painting process. Together with the extraordinarily modern point of view, layout, and proportions of the likeness, and of the style, the subject matter points emphatically in the direction of the sixteenth century. The dress and, specifically, the shape of the decolleté indicate origins no earlier than the 1510s.'[45] The dead sparrow is original, as well as the 'topic, as related to a genre'. He does not advocate for it unequivocally, yet does lean towards it. Then again, he situates the style from 1510 forwards, different to Bob Claessens, for instance, who assumed that it was not worn this way before 1500, but also not after 1510.[46] Weniger sees reworkings in the following places: 'In this way, in terms of painting technique, the especially striking, deep, subtly graduated shadows on the temples and the bodice likewise exhibit overpainting or at least intensifications, like the hands that have been modelled with similar subtlety. The iris and pupils – so definitive for the overall effect and the famous gaze – have also been reworked. The shoulders and outline of the neck were altered after the fact. Taking this step, as well as recreating the background, is connected to the overpainting on the girl's bonnet, which has distorted the (original) sense. The earlier background colour was able to show through the transparent tulle fabric, on the lower left and right – as with the forehead even today. Perceptible even to the naked eye, the earlier process harmonises with the deeper, original shoulder line.'[47] Which overpainting comes from an 'earlier time' – as Sneyers indicated after his examinations during the 1960s – is not distinguished from later restorations in this passage. Differentiation is also necessary in the case of the gaze: According to Sneyers, the iris of the right eye was reworked – is Weniger referring to both eyes? Moreover, his assessment of the reworking of the pupils is based on his own observation, not on the results of the radiography, the way they are documented in the archival file on the picture.[48] Weniger also archived his own slides from the investigation in that dossier. In the slide of the mouth, we see that the shadow was painted over below the lower lip. And on the drawing of the reworked shadows, which Weniger added to the documentation as an overview, it is clear how attempts were made with the shadows to heighten the contrasts in the picture, possibly to the benefit of a higher degree of tension, drama. We recognise these shadows as softly drawn or greyish in the portrait – along the blue border of the bonnet; on the forehead, temples, and cheeks of the child; on the dress in the area of the chest by the left arm; on the right upper arm; in the folds down to the waist; as well as along the left lower arm; and on the left hand. At the same time, this means that the remaining shadows are original. In this way, the shadow going along the left upper arm on the outside complements the light, shadow-free part of the right upper arm on the outside, both of which support the gaze away from the left half of the body. The original arrangement of light and shadow had already been part of the gaze, its direction going into the lighter portion. Certainly, it was less dramatic – as Weniger's slide of the mouth shows – but it was there from the beginning. Thus, the art historian writes: 'Without the shadow having been accentuated after the fact, the portrait would presumably give off a younger appearance.' In this regard, he makes reference to the 'extremely soft transitions from before the overpainting already. In a way that is hardly noticeable, the light pink of the lower lip vanishes into the surrounding flesh tones.'[49]

* * *

First impressions are 'pre-iconographic', as I wrote at the outset, in line with Erwin Panofsky and Max Imdahl. That was our point of departure. The search for iconographic sources brought to light only one possibility: the love poems of Catullus. The spectrum of iconological interpretation, on the other hand, ranged far and wide – does it concern the portrait of a princess, separated from a group likeness? Is it connected with the erotic representations of the genre *Little girl with dead bird*? Or does it have to do with an allegory on life and death, from humanist circles? And, on top of that: Who painted the picture, who reworked it – when and why, in which way? All these questions are still at stake, opening up possible ways of seeing the picture. In the process, the 'historical truth' is shown to be extremely inestimable. What does become clear, though, is the potentiality that has been able to unfold along with the picture historically, as it has been observed since the twentieth century, by art historians, poets, museum-goers. Thus it remains as much a device for historical estimations and potentialities as the picture is today in its 'aesthetic evidence', in the words of Imdahl. This evidence is inscribed in the picture, as a network of formal, visible tensions. It is sustained by looking away from and looking deeper at what? And the way this comes through in the composition of the figures of the girl and the bird as well as the arrangement of light and shadow. With the reworkings this section of the entire picture was changed and that arrangement dramatised – a legacy of Romanticism perhaps, of overpainting in the nineteenth century? All these questions are still open. This is the picture we have got in this condition. And in this state it possesses 'aesthetic evidence'. Seeing it for the first time, 'pre-iconographically', we find only this one certainty in observation, the knowledge of reasonably seeing it again and differently, based on a tension that is peculiar to this picture, and which Max Imdahl called 'iconic'. In this way, with an awareness of these art-historical questions, everyone is asked to observe the picture again and differently in its evidence and potentiality, just as P.C. Boutens did, when he saw it in a new and different way during his time in 1942. In this sense, we face him today, in our time. How would we answer him?

Thoughts on life and death (I)

'Death is the great aporia in the face of which all symbolism fails and in response to which it constitutes itself' – Philippe Forest wrote this sentence in his essay *Tous les enfants sauf un* ('All the children except one').[50] His book is a 'memento mori' to his prematurely deceased daughter. His third souvenir. He wrote two novels about her, then this essay. *All symbolism fails in the face of death – and constitutes itself as an answer to it.* It is humanity's fundamental situation, as Hans Blumenberg describes it: not being able to look past our own situation and yet still having to act.[51] Symbolism – that would be the way of dealing indirectly with it, the ability of opposing helplessness, impotence with anything at all, in a form that remains, that passes away.

Even today, the *Little girl with dead bird* still shows a girl, who perhaps lived until the end of the sixteenth century, but who has since died, well over 400 years ago. In his final written fragments, Paul Ricœur noted: 'I read on an art book cover: *Watteau (1684-1721).*'[52] And he wonders what that means – the name, the dates, the dates in brackets, the transmission of those dates and the name. The name of a famous painter, which likewise stands for his work, a work that transcends the dates in brackets. In another passage, though, he asks about those 'who leave no trace behind (...)'.[53] The girl is unknown, as is the name of the painter. Her picture is a nameless shard, in the midst of a culture that is still familiar, comparable to the nameless evidence preserved in archaeology, the final remains of a distant culture – what was this picture for?

All symbolism fails in the face of death – and constitutes itself as an answer to it. Is that not true of everything that eludes us? That is how phenomenology would pose the question today. Is death not one of many phenomena that define us, one that cannot be grasped and yet becomes perceptible in desiring a response to it? Is it not the child's question, *Where was I before I was born?*, opening up a horizon that becomes only more elusive the more we pursue the question? How far back are the memories of a family carried? Past the great-grandparents? Only rarely indeed. Transitoriness is as invisible as it is massive. Once, when reading a biography on one of the first Hollywood stars – *Rodolfo Valentino*, written by Renate Berger – a virtually forgotten world opened up before me, a world where – only a hundred years ago – Valentino's name was on everyone's tongue, where careers were planned and networks woven, movies made, where audiences went to the cinemas in droves – all over now, over and done with.[54] Shining bright and fading away, coming and going. That is why Hans Blumenberg recalls the purpose of institutions, encapsulated as they are, yet as such surviving and ensuring their use, along with their traces, from generation to generation.[55] The *Little girl with dead bird* found its way into this kind of capsule – the Museums for Fine Arts in Brussels – in which it is preserved and shown.

Symbolism fails in the face of wonder – is it not this phrase that comes to a head in death? It is an ancient topos that philosophy begins in wonder – and practises for death. The wonder of birth, when a child grows from a woman's body, announces itself with labour pains, when the head appears, the woman herself a being with two heads, until all at once the entire body appears, a child *comes into the world*. And then, there it is, with its first breath, reflexes, movements. Even though the parents created it, where the child comes from eludes them, its appearance is wondrous, the way it increasingly occupies, interacts with, determines its own space, showing emotions never expressed in that way before, opening up its thoughts, in interplay with the circumstances, with its parents.

Our own origin eludes us – and our future. So, too, our body: when healthy, when we do not sense its working (the knees bending when we sit, the neck tilting when we look); when ill, when the body escapes this seemingly self-evident state (in pain, discomfort), or even turns against us, even before we sense it (in ulcers, tumours that grow unnoticed).

The way what I have seen eludes me – in what I still know of it, or can remember, or is forgotten, appears to be new, remains vanished.

The way sleep eludes and strengthens me, when I am really settled down, and awakens me again.

The way others – my wife, my daughter – can surprise me again and again, with their uniqueness that eludes me.

All these are examples of temporality, of the course of eluding, transitioning, coming and going. Into these *passages* the answers that we find linger – just as the picture of one moment counters that which eludes coming and going, the *moment*. Only the fraction of a second, fixed in the image. The girl looks up, soon she might say something. Yet she remains mute. The painter only lets the gaze speak – the look of the girl and the observer.

Forest writes: 'There is something universal in the human condition that everywhere and always cares about – from desire and from grief – confrontation with what is really impossible. And the death of a child is one of the faces of that which is impossible.'[56] When one of my wife's colleagues was telling about her cancer, she recalled the words of her doctor who, when she complained about why it had stricken her of all people, said: 'Well, then, what was a girl with leukaemia supposed to say?' The death of a child appears to be the greatest injustice, as if it still had its life ahead of it. The violent death of the bird – a defenceless body, in the hands of the girl.

* * *

'For the sake of the children/that we still are,/fairy tales have happy endings' – a verse by Wisława Szymborska, from her poem "Into the ark", translated by Stanislaw Baranczak and Claire Cavanagh.[57] Once when I was leafing through Grimm's fairytales with my daughter, my gaze fell upon a story that was no longer familiar to me, and I read it aloud, unsuspectingly. The piece was called "The Companionship of Cat and Mouse",[58] not quite two pages long. I started reading: 'A cat and mouse wanted to live together, so they set up a common household.' Cat and Mouse moved in together, and among their provisions shared a little jar of fat, hidden in a church. Making excuses, Cat sneaked out of the house, first licking up the skin from the top of the fat, then half the jar, and finally the whole thing. 'However, soon winter came and there was nothing more to be found outside. So the mouse said to the cat, "Come, let's go to our supply that we stuck beneath the altar in the church."' When they get to the jar, though, and Mouse sees that it is empty, she suspects Cat's treachery, wants to say something, but 'No sooner did she say it than the cat jumped on her and swallowed her in one gulp.'[59] – for, as the original German version of the tale concludes, 'That's the way it goes in the world.'[60] It was this last sentence that completely upset my daughter. All at once, the pleasant afternoon storytime had taken a disconcerting turn. To have the tale end with something terrifying – that was just too much for her. She did not want to hear any more stories from that book, and I was sorry for having ruined the good mood we were in with it.

For the sake of the children that we still are, fairy tales have happy endings. I was sorry, because I did not believe the ending myself and did not want her to think that I agreed with it. The world is not eating and being eaten. Joie de vivre always extends back into childhood, into play, forgetting ourselves, and pleasure; sharing that joy with my daughter would always be more important to me than the self-righteousness of any cynical vision of the world. That also means that a 'happy ending' is not taken for granted. *For the sake of the children that we still are, fairy tales have happy endings.* This 'happy ending' is one belonging to fairytales and stories. As pure ideals, however, they do not find their way into experience. As Adorno noted, for example, in his *Aesthetic Theory*: 'Experiences are not "as if".'[61] The experience of reading and imagining – imagination, that is – is itself not fictive. In this case, the 'happy ending' is mixed with its imaginability. It is only imaginable, even as an idealised form, if it appears plausible. It is constantly interwoven with experience – moments of happiness, of light-heartedness, which suddenly overtake or overtook us, when we were able to keep our balance, for example, on a bicycle, when a touch was responded to, a look was returned with a smile. The 'happy ending' might conclude a story, one that for the most part only appears to be one that is told, for the experienced moments that reinforce us do not demand any conclusion. *Stopping when something is at its best?* Who would end a love or a friendship that way? A career perhaps, if we notice that it is no longer sustainable. A relationship, though, has another quality. Stopping when it has outlived itself seems to be the more commensurate variation in this case.

Szymborska's verse reminds adults that they cannot simply set themselves up in a bitter vision of the world without denying their own origins, their own joie de vivre. And this thought extends farther than any theory of repression. It does not only revolve around a conflict between the cynic and the analyst. It is about becoming unbelievable ourselves, when we are incapable of giving any sense to a 'happy ending', to 'good' as the final word of the original verse – for others *and* ourselves. Which vision do you offer the girl could likewise be a question to the observer, in Brussels, in the Museums of Fine Arts. What may we hope for, we could ask together with Kant, and the one to whom hope appears to be too self-indulgent can perhaps change the question, as does Rudolf Boehm, into: *What can we do?* (For, as he writes, 'we may only hope of being in the position to see what we have to know, to understand what we are supposed to do, and to bring about what we are able to create.'[62]) The picture is a philosophical challenge as well. It has survived the time of its creation; it adorns the handy museum guide just as it does postcards and notebooks; it lends itself to popularisation, advertising; and it has its permanent place in the exhibition hall of the Old Masters collection. The question as to popularisation is one for *our* time. Answering it is in line with the way of reading *historically*, as its pendant and first point of reference. In so doing, the philosophical challenge is one of representation and theme: The preserved image poses the question of meaning for life and death (what does that say about its reception?). And it poses it vehemently, in the shape of the young girl. We cannot evade this question by escaping into being a know-it-all. The subject matter eludes any delimitation or determination capable of being closed off. Yet that is precisely why it is disturbing, constantly pulling us in when we do not confront that unease, which is to say: when we do not respond to our desire for dealing with it on our own and do not find our own way of dealing with it. Ultimately, this unease cannot be exorcised: the fear of death, which already lies dormant in becoming aware of the fact that we have to leave everything at some point. Emmanuel Levinas may indeed remark: 'The unknown of death, which is not given straight off as nothingness but is correlative to an experience of the impossibility of nothingness (...).'[63] Yet the experience of the impossibility of nothingness, of that *everythingness* that I must leave, including my self, will be physically broken – that much is certain; and the breach of my integrity will breach the *everythingness* from which the 'experience of the impossibility of nothingness' is nourished. There is still no solace to associate with it.

Yet do we have need of solace? As a Protestant, too, Ricœur asked himself this question in a critical way. In his fragment about Jacques

Derrida, he wrote: 'I take the same starting point: what I do not believe. If "learning finally how to live" is to learn to die, to take into account accepting absolute mortality without salvation, resurrection, or redemption, I share all the negative here. I, too, do not expect resurrection for myself (...).'[64] And he makes note of his reasons: 'In the first place, I object to everything make-believe about a (survival) of (?) the survival of (others). I survive on borrowed time.'[65] After the catastrophes of the twentieth century, it is untenable in the Christian faith to imagine ourselves as elect, as protected for an 'eternal life' vis-à-vis those who were persecuted and killed unjustly. That injustice demands human solidarity, with the victims. 'I survive on borrowed time' recalls the outcome, life, being on borrowed time. Not that a prison would be waiting at the other end – but instead death's immeasurable necessity, its absoluteness. Life is not a punishment that we supposedly have 'on borrowed time', nor is death a judgement of the elect and the outcast. In the very first place, being on borrowed time is a kind of prolonging. A postponement, a forgetting that ebbs and flows, an undulation that dissipates in silence and comes again to life. In line with Vladimir Jankélévitch, Ricœur described it as follows, in his study *Memory, history, forgetting*: 'No one can make it the case that what is no longer has not been. The forgetting which, according to Heidegger, conditions remembering is related to the past as having-been. We comprehend the apparent paradox if, by forgetting, we understand an immemorial resource and not an inexorable destruction.'[66] Two thoughts intersect with each other here. On the one hand: You *have* lived – nothing can render this life undone (and it has also been bracketed: *Watteau, 1684- 1721*). On the other hand: Forgetting *conditions* remembering. Thus, only those who have passed through forgetting will be remembered, the sentence seems to mean. Art history offers multiple examples, for instance, of constantly being remembered anew, based on the *work*. Yet what about those 'who leave no trace behind', as Ricœur remarks?[67] The 'idea of the trace that passes through my own'[68], can it not also mean acting in the sense given by Hannah Arendt, the solidarity of being politically engaged, across generations? Still, what about those *who leave no trace behind*? The enormous, vehement invisibility of our closest relatives, who two, three generations later have already vanished, whose graves were dispersed, whose memories are expired? We can grasp this expiration as a moment of natural becoming – the one makes room for the other. For believers, human beings may be just 'dust', yet those who, like Aristotle, understand humankind to be classified amid the pigeonholes of living creatures – with plants and animals – will never deny what is creaturely about human beings. Even so, it seems human to see ourselves constantly in what is more creaturely, and to experience our own impotence as painful, whenever the loss of another, of someone close, is expressed in dealing with this impotence symbolically, in the rituals and trappings of burial, the way these have been handed down since prehistoric times. Of the 'notion of the trace that lives on in my people', Ricœur writes: 'A thought comes back to me: "the hope that she will survive me". All of the religious is there, as a link between my wanting to live and my own.'[69] *Hope* – when Rudolf Boehm puts it in brackets, then that comes from a scepticism that will become clear in the context of these present considerations. For Ricœur, though, this hope remains the epitome of those who are altogether religious – when nothing is capable of preserving any traces of mine, when my actions have been extinguished in the gruesomeness of what has gone on, when all memory eludes human beings, does every notion of the Other expire with that then? And would the excessive extreme of this notion be – God? Here the philosophical idea takes a turn, into an extreme kind of speculation. Perhaps, though, it is also only the desire showing through with which we searched for a philosophical, bona fide answer – a desire that constantly overshoots the answers, that only searches in the answer for a *way of dealing*, when the subject matter does not comply with any classification.

In 1971, Primo Levi published a story with the title "In the park". It is the wondrous story of a park where literary characters live, so long as they are being remembered by readers. In writing an autobiography, one author attempts to change himself into a character who would be granted life in this park of literature. As a well-known author, he is successful in becoming loved by readers, and so he finds entry into the park. He gets to know the great figures of literature personally, and even one of his own characters keeps him company. Then forgetting sets in, and the characters fade away. And one day the author notices this paleness on himself, and it becomes more and more overt, makes him turn transparent, until he fades away: 'When, in mid-June, he realized he could see the chair he was sitting on, and the grass under his feet, Antonio understood that his time had come: the memory of him was extinct and his testimony complete. He felt sadness, but neither fear nor anguish. He took leave of James and his new friends, and sat under an oak to wait for his flesh and spirit to dissolve into light and wind.'[70]

* * *

As Rudolf Boehm says in his prologue to his *Kritik der Grundlagen des Zeitalters* ('Critique of the foundations of the epoch') from 1973: 'In the end, though, nothing at all is lost with the loss of hopes and expectations, only freedom regained. For, as far as humanity is concerned, nothing good or useful is to be hoped or expected. There is only doing and providing.'[71] He belongs to the same generation as Ricœur and Levi. His thinking, too, plays against the backdrop of the catastrophes of the twentieth century. Disillusionment speaks from his critical thinking, a disillusionment that only gives any credit to 'doing' and 'providing'. He, too, is concerned with an answer for that little word 'good', the 'happy ending' that was previously discussed with a view to Szymborska's poetry. And what is good does not stand apart from what is useful, even if it cannot be reduced to usefulness. It subsequently becomes clear which focus matters to Boehm: humanity. What, then, are we *to know, to do*, and *what are we able to create*, in the sense of the Aristotelian distinction between theory, praxis, and practice; of observation, action, and production; of philosophy, the art of living, and technology? 'And what is it, then, that we have to know?' he writes at the beginning of his *Poietik* ('Poetics', 2005): 'If I am to answer this question in only two words, I can say: We have to understand that un-human Nature is not quite kindly disposed towards human beings (…). The universe (…) is obviously even hostile towards life, up to the planets that are our neighbours, with which we share a common sun. Yet Nature has filled even our life-loving planet Earth with not only hospitable mountains and valleys, forests, fields, and meadows, but also stormy seas, glowing-hot deserts, ice-cold steppes, and impassable mountain ranges and weather conditions that are not hospitable at all.'[72] The message is unambiguous: We are alone in the universe, and even on earth we can only live on continents, and not even everywhere there. That is our space for living. And we would do well to take this limitation as our point of departure so as to accommodate ourselves with an awareness of our responsibility. That is the tenor of his *Poietik*, of his thinking ever since the *Kritik der Grundlagen des Zeitalters*. And it is an incontrovertible fact. There is no second world.

Ever since Ludwig Feuerbach, the latter idea has been at odds with any postulation of the religious, as represented by Ricœur, for instance (we ought not put it any more mildly, if we are familiar with the intensity of the discussions concerning precisely this issue[73]). Its most striking formulation is found in Friedrich Nietzsche's *Antichrist*: 'In Christianity neither morality nor religion has even a single point of contact with reality. Nothing but imaginary *causes* ("God," "soul," "ego," "spirit," "free will" – for that matter, "unfree will"), nothing but imaginary *effects* ("sin," "redemption," "grace," "punishment," "forgiveness of sins"). Intercourse between imaginary beings ("God," "spirits," "souls"); an imaginary *natural* science (anthropocentric; no trace of any concept of natural causes); an imaginary *psychology* (nothing but self-misunderstandings, interpretations of agreeable or disagreeable general feelings – for example, of the states of the *nervus sympathicus* – with the aid of the sign language of the religio-moral idiosyncrasy: "repentance," "pangs of conscience," "temptation by the devil," "the presence of God"); an imaginary *teleology* ("the kingdom of God," "the Last Judgment," "eternal life"). This *world of pure fiction* is vastly inferior to the world of dreams insofar as the latter *mirrors* reality, whereas the former falsifies, devalues, and negates reality. Once the concept of "nature" had been invented as the opposite of "God," "natural" had to become a synonym of "reprehensible": this whole world of fiction is rooted in *hatred* of the natural (of reality!); it is the expression of a profound vexation at the sight of reality. *But this explains everything.* Who alone has good reason *to lie his way out* of reality? He who *suffers* from it. But to suffer from reality is to be a piece of reality *that has come to grief.* The preponderance of feelings of displeasure over feelings of pleasure is the *cause* of this fictitious morality and religion' (...).'[74] On the one hand, Nietzsche's tirade sounds trenchant and probably even liberating for some; however, it is continually fuelled by the binary of true and false, and only in such a way that Christian doctrine, which negates 'Nature', is in turn negated back to 'reality' by the text's author. Yet any dialectical counter-attack does not escape being dialectically related back, much as atheism does not escape belief. That is not an argument for believing but, rather, it shows that the counter-attack derives from the same logical preconditions that it is fighting against. For any philosopher of the mind, that is a truism. Adorno and Sartre therefore attempted it with forms of a 'negative dialectics', in order to get out of this back-and-forth game *by means of* the dialectic. It appears to be much more promising, however, to expand the framework of the dialectic by means of genuinely different concepts. That was precisely what Maurice Merleau-Ponty was working on, when he sought to split up dialectical oppositions based on structures (ever since his first treatise *The Structure of behavior*), or when he introduced thinking of a figure/ground constellation from Gestalt psychology into his *Phenomenology of perception*, that is, thinking of an irreversible relationship: Only by way of the figure does its ground visually appear, not vice versa. That is not a dialectical relationship, which is made to operate like two extreme opposites running into each other, the way light and dark are able to merge into each another across the spectrum of colour; and which also does not consist of the opposition of two things that exclude each other categorically and assert themselves autonomously – like the purported opposition of life and death (in accordance with the Epicurean adage: 'If you are, it is not; if it is, you are not'[75]). With Merleau-Ponty's work, then, we can thoroughly call Nietzsche's dialectical opposition into question, as when the phenomenologist writes: '[O]ne cannot judge the powers of life by those of death, nor define without arbitrariness life as the sum of the forces that resist death (...).'[76] Along with Heidegger, Ricœur had recalled that forgetting is the necessary precondition for remembering. To what extent is death part of life? This question is what Merleau-Ponty poses.

The dialectical inversion of belief into a vehement atheism thus does not appear to me to be very convincing, if we remain a child of the same logic. Atheistic 'revelations' like those of Feuerbach, Marx, or Nietzsche do not tell us more than the previously already invalidated 'proofs of God' (and the Nietzsche citation demonstrates that he is likewise operating dialectically). Here, whether belief or 'ideal', there is no proof, only *having an opinion*. I doubt the content of this having an opinion less than the constantly identical dialectical schematic in which it is composed. This schematic is a construction that does not do any justice to 'life' per se – in the way Merleau-Ponty indicates – and, as such, not to the relationship of life and death, either.

Nevertheless, it is not as simple as that; I hear this objection from reading other philosophers – like Ernst Tugendhat, for instance, who similarly does not see Christian belief as being in tune with any form of being intellectually bona fide. In that regard, three decisive and path-breaking questions arise at this juncture: One fundamentally concerns the relationship to that 'belief', the other the relationship between life and death, and the third whether and how both questions are related to each other.

* * *

First of all, as to the first of the three questions: Which insights make any 'bona fide nature' of belief difficult – and what might speak in favour of 'belief'?

How do we want to live? This question is inevitably posed in considering what Tugendhat calls the *proximity of death* ('*Todesnähe*') – that is, not the abstract thought of dying *at all* or *at some time*, even not the fear of pain that can rise to the level of a phobia towards death. It is instead the profound uncertainty in the idea of *soon*, in which a *not yet* is always expressed, a deferral, a wanting *to live* more, even though nobody could imagine living *forever*, here 'on earth'. The proximity of death means not only our own mortal danger but just as much the experience of when a 'part of me' dies, is extinguished, disappears with the death of another. When I myself can no longer experience what I was able to share with that person. The proximity of death already becomes familiar to us in our family when a relative dies, our own grandparents, not even to mention existentially unsettling experiences like the death of a parent, for example.[77] The proximity of death, then, puts us before the question of possibly dealing with these events. When Blumenberg described humanity's fundamental situation as not being able to look past our own situation and yet having to deal with it, this compulsion to act leads to differentiating amongst modes of cognition, namely, those that allow for dealing directly to those dealing only indirectly with our own situation – life between birth and death. Directly, for instance, in that scientific knowledge makes intervention in our own situation possible like, for example, when a heart transplant succeeds; indirectly, when this is aspired to as a *possibility*; radically indirectly, when any intervention appears to be pointless, since we are not able to create our own living conditions en masse ourselves – perhaps we are able to make animals become extinct, yet we cannot make evolution happen in the laboratory; we can pollute the air, but we cannot produce it. Nature still appears in these terms and preconditions. And they also concern our mortality, as the price for procreation by means of conception. Seen from a purely biological perspective, death is as old as life: 500 million years.[78] Dealing with what is radically indirect, with our preconditions – and the list of these conditions since time immemorial is long, extending to everything that eludes our grasp above and beyond any limitation – can only happen *symbolically*. Even so, as a symbolic share of the entire spectrum of attempted and partially resolved dealings with our own situation, our grasp has a limit. Rituals, religions, forms of art constitute the one extreme end of dealing with what is radically indirect, while the pure sciences fix the other extreme end of direct interference. Both ends open up latitude for acting within our own behaviour, between that which can be changed, on the one hand, and that which does not let go of humanity as such, that which concerns our own preconditions by which we act and which we do not fully find ourselves, on the other hand. Tugendhat also speaks of the fact 'that the need for a belief in gods is not only a cultural but, rather, an anthropological phenomenon grounded in the structure of being human, on the one hand, but that it is impossible for humanity today to yield to this need, unless we deceive ourselves'.[79] The question, then, is: Why? What distinguishes humanity today – clinging to the same anthropological preconditions as our predecessors, and having to live and die in our own manner – from those very predecessors?

Being bona fide means taking compelling reasons seriously. Rudolf Boehm, for instance, sketches a clear picture of the Christian doctrine of salvation, which I would like to cite here in extenso: 'It is a doctrine of redemption. Redemption from what? "From the law of sin and death". Death, which is "the wages of sin". The happy message of Christ says: God's punishment – the punishment of death – for the human transgression of God's command, for eating from the tree of the knowledge of good and evil and wanting to become like God, has been lifted. On what path? On the way of grace. Humanity has been released from its punishment, forgiven its sin, by grace. It has even been promised access to the tree of life and re-entry into God's paradise. The only condition to which the divine act of grace has been linked, should humanity want to share in that grace, is that humanity recognises this grace as grace (and not as its 'right'), that it confesses its guilt and, in fact, has thoroughly forfeited its punishment, and repents: "Repent, for the kingdom of heaven is near," is therefore literally what the Gospel says. Of course, God could not lift this judgement over humanity, which had wanted to overstep the bounds between humanity and God, just with the stroke of a pen, as it were. An act, an extraordinary deed of God was required: for lifting these bounds on his own by overstepping them himself. It is in Christ that God has indeed taken the sin of humanity upon himself: The fact that humanity wanted to become God is now repaid by God's love in that God himself becomes human. God's love repays the fact that humanity wanted to be like God, and thus free from death, by God himself taking death upon himself in human form. God suffers death, humanity gains eternal life. God dies, humanity will live in immortality. The bounds between God and humanity are (...) lifted. The ancient discord between God (the gods) and humanity are overcome by the love of God, a god who thus for the first time no longer appears as a jealous (...), albeit righteous god, as the object of godliness, but who instead becomes kind, and kind in such a way that the divine love for humanity, the human love for God, and the love of human beings for one another coalesces into a single love that embraces the world. Familial relationships now prevail between God and humanity, produced in all kinds of ways by a sort of marriage between God and Mary: God is the father, God's son is also a 'son of man', a human son, and through him all human beings are God's children.'[80]

Belief is a form of activity. The praxis of belief, experience, is not identical to its formulation. And yet it must be measured by this formulation, since Scripture has expanded the ritual. It is now, then, that the work of exegesis, of interpretation, begins. What does 'sin' mean? And what about 'law'? Is it the recognition of good and evil, which defines God as such? Why is this divine characteristic available to humanity, yet denying it to humanity requires the use of violence – punishment by death? Which violence grants the knowledge of good and evil? And why does God grant humanity grace, when it is nevertheless vanquished? Because humanity is his 'in his image'? An image of the distinction between what is true, God, and what is false, the copy? The copy possesses no 'right' – it is a testimonial, an attestation of what is true. 'Know this truth!', and the 'right relationship' will again prevail in the 'House of the Lord' …

As Jan Assmann has written, for Christianity – though for Judaism and Islam as well – 'the order that founds human coexistence is not of this world but flows from an extramundane source'.[81] This source appears even outside the 'cosmos', that is, beyond this organism that made possible life on earth as a constellation in space. And *at the same time* this source must appear as a personal god, as a force that 'cares about humanity'. An 'unmoved mover', source of all energy, and *father* all in one. In infinity, time and space may not play any role. For human beings, however, the more than 2000 years since revelation are no less distant than the astronomical figures for space, as recalled by Lars Gustafsson: 'Observing the starry heaven means seeing into the past. Most of the stars we can recognise with the naked eye are more than ten light years away. Our local galaxy with its many hundreds of billions of stars has a diameter of 100,000 light years. The nearest other galaxy, the Andromeda Nebula, is two million light years distant. In the far distance, fifty million light years away, is a formation our local portion belongs to, and which comprises more than 500,000 galaxies.'[82] The way the Swedish poet-philosopher speaks of what is 'local' is beautiful, as if there were this framework when gazing at the stardust into which we have dived. Even when the cosmonauts on *Sputnik* communicated that there was supposedly no god in space, the effect was self-aggrandising and arrogant, of course, like a potshot during the Cold War. And, similarly, there are believers who wipe all these figures from the table with one sweep – what do they even mean, in comparison with *God*, who is superior to all comparison? Where, though, is humaneness in this distance? The distance into the past, distance into space? The gaze into the distance – for the girl in our picture, it is just looking up. In her times, the starry heaven was still one belonging to a 'cosmos', for which God was responsible, as God the Creator. Today, though, the 'cosmos' is scattered into distances, into infinite expanses that turn us humans into such marginal oddities that in a movie like *Midnight in Paris*, for instance, the protagonist may once again marvel at whether it would not be unbelievable that somewhere in this universe a city like Paris might be shining.[83]

The miracle is this *in spite of everything*. That is how it appears at least, in our dealing with the *radically alien, radically distant*.

'God' and the 'cosmos' have infinitely diverged. The principle of unity *and* unity. They had constituted the 'divine unity of the world', as it was celebrated in the name of many gods. It is the infinite distance that remains –

'Infinity's ends fused quickly./(...)//There wasn't a moment to lose,/no deferred questions, no belated revelations,/(...)/Life, however long, will always be short./Too short for anything to be added.' – Wisława Szymborska, in her poem "Our ancestors' short lives".[84]

Infinity's ends – *we*. We cannot imagine our own ends, *nor* our infinity. Are we the ends of this infinity? Manifestations, moved movers, concentrated bodies, *physis*, in Nature –

'Death / always arrives (...) too late. // (...) As far as you've come, / can't be undone.'[85]

These manifestations, in the whirlpool of becoming – passing away, following our own traces ...

'Day to day I trust in permanence,/in history's prospects./(...)//When writing these lines,/I wonder,/what in them/will come to sound ridiculous and when.//Fear strikes me only at times./On the road./In a strange city.'[86]

'The joy of writing./The power of preserving./Revenge of a mortal hand.'[87]

'Tickets to the afterlife are paid/by our collective memory./(…) Every day/some dead man's banished from eternity.'[88]

Primo Levi, "In the park"

* * *

Whether the poetess knew the picture with the girl and the dead sparrow? In her volume entitled *A Large number* (1976), she writes in her poem "In Praise of my sister": 'Holds in her hands a baby sparrow with a broken wing (…).'[89] Is the wing in the picture broken? The sparrow has been injured on its throat and wing. The association with the sparrow in hand is only one of many that describe a woman, under the pressure of expectations of her to adopt a stance in simply behaving. After the words 'Young, young as ever, still looking young' comes the allusion to the 'sparrow with a broken wing'. It is not clear whether the personal pronoun continues to describe her as an adult woman or as a recollection of her as a little girl. A grammatical shift in gender would not necessarily be needed for that, even if it were required in linguistic terms, strictly speaking. 'Woman', however, has always been feminine, in the way grammar intentionally compels us. Formal logic is not gender-neutral, either, as Luce Irigaray insisted. And inasmuch as she barely finds her stance, grammatical confusion would be only one of many disorientations. She is a she, whether as a girl or as a woman. 'Holds in her hands a baby sparrow with a broken wing'. Amid all her pragmatism, perseverance, this shows her only fragility. A female perspective on the picture might also say: You will still become a woman, and how will you do so? Not only being a child is fragile, but also being a little girl. The sparrow 'with a broken wing' appears in this way like the continuation of the motif of lost innocence, in literature. Perhaps Szymborska knew one of the examples of *Little girl with dead bird*? Or is it her own reading of Catullus she evokes in this case? And if innocence were not meant at all sexually, but instead related to trust, to feeling safe? The poetic image splits the meanings up.

Intercultural comparisons

The 'bona fide nature of belief' – *what would argue for it?* Ernst Tugendhat says that, if anyone would still take it seriously to be a source of inspiration, then it would only be 'to preserve a certain respectability vis-à-vis those who believe',[90] in contrast to atheism. Is atheism an alternative, though? Jan Assmann writes that the trauma of belief in an exclusive god is based on a two-fold murder of God, 'first of all the "pagan" gods and then the god of monotheism himself. The theoclastic violence that inheres within monotheism, that is to say, is ultimately directed against God himself'.[91] Atheism inheres in monotheism and does not denote a position outside of any metaphysical tradition. François Jullien demonstrates this very vividly in his book *Du «temps». Éléments d'une philosophie du vivre* ('On "time". Elements of a philosophy of living'). By way of introduction, I would like to sketch his fundamental thoughts here, in order to use them as a point of departure for discussing possible intercultural dimensions of the picture.[92]

As the French Sinologist Jullien puts it, 'The expression "What meaning does life have?" reveals the metaphysical plane of our thinking still in the midst of the current, everyday manner of speaking.'[93] Why? To start, he argues in regard of the stockpile of languages. Can the expression be translated, for instance, into Chinese? 'In Classical Chinese we find nothing that would come close to it (instead only the "destiny/lot" of life, *sheng-ming*); and

I would hardly know how to translate into modern Chinese which meaning life has (unless I would graft a new meaning on; I vacillate between which "significance" (*yisi*)? or which "importance" (*yiyi*)? or which "value" (*jiazhi*)? or which "goal" (*mudi*)?).'[94] Yet the 'meaning of life' concerns not only its 'significance', the denotation of something is not identical with its meaning, and its 'value' apparently has to be 'measured' – though life cannot be determined in purely quantitative terms – and it remains to be explained which interpretation the word 'goal' demands, for it is derives from modern Chinese, whereas in Classical Chinese only 'destiny/fate' appears to be an option for the translator. The 'meaning of life', though, is something different to the 'destiny of life' – for what keeps 'meaninglessness' from not also appearing to be 'destiny'?

Since time immemorial in the West, 'destiny' has appeared as what determines persons and what they cannot change. As we read in Pindar, 'time passes', *chronos herpon*, 'passing time'. He cannot arrest time, the sand in the hourglass inevitably runs out, from the top to the bottom, life writes our days off, *until*. And it is at this point where 'metaphysics' begins, whether as ontology, as the philosophical doctrine of the conditions for our Being ('Sein'); or as theology, as the doctrine of the divine conditions for our being. If the question regarding the 'meaning of life' reveals the 'metaphysical plane' even in our day-to-day language, then Jullien sees an absolute connection between the Western question regarding 'meaning' and that of 'time'.

And he again draws attention to the solely linguistic distinctions between, on the one hand, the Ancient Greek and Latin that have become so significant for us and, on the other hand, Classical Chinese: Chinese does not have any conjugations and, in that regard, it does not have to distinguish any grammatical tenses, any *times*. It is without ending and is expressed 'in a kind of "infinitive", to put it in our terms'.[95] For this reason it has also never formed definite articles, that is, they do not speak of 'the' present as such, but as 'present is coming' (*jin-lai*); it is in progress, in the act of becoming.

For in this regard Chinese also does not have any verb corresponding to 'to be', with which 'the being of this present' could be formed. According to Jullien, 'Being' was never part of Chinese language or thought, though 'Becoming' totally is.

Ancient Greek and Latin, on the other hand, conjugate in times of the past, present, and future. And it seems reasonable to ask, whether this very occurrence did not encourage the question regarding *the time*, one time that connects them all. Beginning with Aristotle, the question was emphatically posed. What does it mean, though, with a view towards *life*, Jullien asks. That life *passes away*? That we are supposed to live *in the present*? What, then, characterises *the present*? As in 'prae-esse', being-before ('Davor-sein') – 'we need a *something* (*id*), which "presents itself" and is before that.'⁹⁶ The 'metaphysical plane' appears anew, as a grammatical necessity for determining its own precondition: *the* Being that 'presents itself', or, in the theological sense, the divine. In Bernhard Waldenfels' phenomenology of responsivity, the attempt is made to grasp this 'presents itself' immemorially, as from *itself*, and no longer appearing before a noun, before something substantive. Rather, it appears as the difference of a desire to respond to eluding, from the becoming of eluding, of escaping – temporally, spatially, physically, and bodily – yet in doing so only attaining, realising one's own desire; and in that way, in dealing with the becoming, a Self finds its limits for latitude and activity, with the reflexive forms of *itself* (*ipse*) and *self* (in the sense of 'I myself ...').⁹⁷ According to Jullien, though, these forms cannot be connected to traditional Chinese thought, either – change supposedly never denotes 'something changing itself'.⁹⁸

The fundamental question with a view to life that comes up here is: How do we think this *Becoming*? Arising and passing away, coming and going? In which context? If the 'dramatisation' of life, as 'tragic', is a Western/cultural phenomenon, can it be relativised in adopting other ways of seeing? Or to which standpoint does a way *out of* this alternative lead?

Traditional Chinese thought, according to Jullien, describes the Becoming in Nature as coming from breathing, in the sense of continual interactions between the energies of *yin* (contraction) and *yang* (expansion), as the fundamental contrast of all 'correlated *factors*, constituted as polar opposites (...)'.[99] In this regard, it involves thinking of structures that arise and go away in a correlative way, characterised by the following, fundamental movements: by going away and coming (*zhou*), between the four cardinal directions as well as above and below (*yu*), to which the way (*tao*) proceeds in crisscross fashion, 'though no one knows where.'[100] The constant in the entire matter, the *way*, is not divided from the eternal as the temporal is (whether in the way's independence from it or in its detachment). Rather, the way manifests itself *'throughout* what is changing'. In this sense, there is no world possible outside this world, like in theological thinking; the world manifests itself *immanently* – it was not created ('prae-esse'), is not a 'work', not a 'goal' that is reached; it knows no 'end' and thus no beginning, either. In this way, this world is also not *oriented*, towards something (its end, God, etc.), and orientation also does not determine the thinking of it.[101] It is much more the question of *regulating* that plays a central role. How is the *way* regulated? By an 'economy of the whole', as Jullien writes, which follows the moment like a collection, like a collection of forces, like the contraction of a transition, of renewed opening. He quotes the Taoist thinker Zhuangzi and his *living in adapting*. In Nature, the four seasons are the example: The concept of them (*si shi*, the 'four seasons') comes from the character for moment and occasion (*shi*). The moment and the occasion are always bound to the situation, and every situation contains tendencies towards its change. Every season, according to Jullien, 'integrates (...) in a global way the unsurmountable, indeed unforeseeable variability of the weather, of the *temps qu'il fait*, into that logic, which (alternatingly) allows for the continuity of time passing away, of the *temps qui passe*. And this process throughout the season is in no way regular but, rather, *regulated* (...)'.[102] In thinking the seasons, then, spring and autumn are given precedence, as moments and occasions that mark time and enliven us. As the Sinologist Jullien remarks, their process is thus spoken of as a rhythm, as an 'alternation'.

A moment, therefore, is not just a 'blink of an eye'.[103] The seasons as four moments in the year are contractions, intensifications, for regenerating duration, process. They are not separated from one another but, rather, infinite; and it is only in this respect, according to Jullien, that life finds its 'dimension of endlessness'. The seasons constitute occasions in the sense of 'occurrence', of *living in adapting*, but not in their ignorance (we do not issue any commands to heaven). Comparable to breathing, they cannot be anticipated and do not retain anything, are comprised only of themselves, and are thoroughly situational.

Now, then, which 'elements of a philosophy of living' – Éléments d'une philosophie du vivre, as Jullien calls his book in the subtitle – accompany this way of thinking? Elements for living today as well?

In *living in adapting* – according to the author – following the occurrence of a situation, changing, going along with it in accordance with its tendency means 'in no way being carried along with it; it requires an inner rigour, because otherwise opportunity degenerates into opportunism. The problem, then, is thinking of this following neither weakly nor passively'.[104] Doing so, once again, we need to bear the grammatical structures in mind: In Chinese there is no explication of active and passive according to individual cases. In this regard it is not *one* pole that demands activity, the unilateral initiative, comparable to the Latin subject that is opposed to an object, and which is thought of as active vis-à-vis its passive object. According to Ancient Chinese thought, individuations are much more due to those sources, that *fund* of immanence, and the individuations only exist in integrating with it. Here, too, breath is the central motif: There is no difference between air and breath. Air is not absorbed by breath; there is no possession, no supply. It only takes minutes for a person to die. At no moment is humanity more than its element.

The 'inner rigour' of the individual does not apply to his *orientation* but, rather, to the continual *regulation*, using the moments of transitions in the persistent change in his situations with their respective tendencies – in the best case, without exerting his own force, conveyed by the change that allows us to *live*, in being present in that change. What applies to regulating are the directions that we follow – in that way, what it is about is always known and is not supposed in a possible 'secret', in a hidden 'sense'. It is about the constant renewal of that rest, of the collecting that is connected with *living*, with restful, deep breath. And in that regard it is about moments, transitions, as phases of collecting, contracting, intensifying. Each and every moment 'becomes really specific only as a result of its quality, and it is precisely in this respect that the season of the year is related'.[105] In this way intensification does not mean ex-stasy, stepping outside one's self – and in this sense, it does not mean 'event', either, as an extraordinary break with what is usual, what is known: '(...) the least "extraordinary" moments can also be the deepest: they "collect" most of all (...): this moment can be the one in which we exchange precisely these words, or the walk on which these words are spoken, or – even more comprehensively – the stay at the seaside during which this walk took place...'.[106] In Western thinking, Jullien readily sees points of contact for this notion, for living in the moment of the occasion – and not in the 'timeframe of the present' – under a catchphrase that he borrows from Michel de Montaigne, which Montaigne employs at the end of his *Essais*: 'living à propos'. At first glance, it possesses the same grammatically infinite nature that Chinese thinking demands. And in lieu of 'prae-esse', of a 'being before', it sets forth a 'posed before' ('propositum'), which can be interpreted as something 'proposed', 'proffered', 'propounded', 'propositioned', as a condition yet also as the occasion of a situation. Furthermore, à propos is a formulaic *transitional* phrase, in the sense of à propos, I also wanted to tell you ...

And this formulation speaks explicitly of *living* – and not of metaphysically informed alternatives like 'existing', for instance. And because 'ex-sistence' is conceived *outside* one's self, as a shift *away from* one's self, according to Jullien, the 'possibility of any (moment of the world) coming to one's self [is] suppressed from the outset'.[107] *Living à propos*, then, would mean: Every moment has its occasion, *in* deepening, collecting, not in the decision for it but in surrendering to it, whereby no beginning can be 'made' but, rather, a moment in the intensification of the infinite is able to appear, the proverbial feeling: *to live*.

With *living* understood in this way, how, then, is death portrayed? The individual is not opposed as the subject to an object, to the world; he does not ex-sist or in-sist, is not determined by his initiative; he does not grasp his birth as a beginning, his life as a line. It is not the extra-ordinary – whether ontologically as an 'event' or theologically as a 'miracle' – that informs his understanding of the world; in distinction to rupture, revolution, revelation, he thinks constantly from the perspective of *immanence* – Nature constitutes the 'fund' of life, of shapes, the 'foundation' of its 'characters'; Nature's immanence only *turns out* to be, only *is proved*, yet never itself comes to light, remaining radically hidden and in that way effective; and because this radical immanence is never able to become explicit, only a commensurate way of dealing with it can be sought, though never any *proposition* for it that would supposedly apply to a question about *meaning*; the question about the 'meaning of life' falls short of life, just as the question of death fails death.

The reality of death leads anew into the radical immanence of Nature. *Adapting*, up to the 'last moment', means *dealing with, interacting until the end*, in breathing, in the coincidence of all life. Dealing means: the ways of dealing, moments of finding breath, rhythms. Air closes off where breath expires, where it is no longer sustained by it, whisps away. Water closes off around what has sunken away. Jullien cites Wang Fuzhi: '(…) when (…) "things no longer work", when the flow stagnates, instead of "proceeding", then we despair and become "full of cares"'.¹⁰⁸ Dealing with death does not depend on something other, something outside, but instead leads into the power of immanence, and encountering it supposedly has to do with dealing to the level of carelessness (*wu you*), which concept when given a positive turn would be that of evolution (*you*). In this way, once again, the loss of our own individuation is thought primarily to be *transition, in whatever direction*, for it is not about orientation, only about the regulation of further becoming, and that alternating state is part of the 'harmony' of becoming, the going that is connected to coming, the dying that is bound to living. Jullien concludes his observations by noting, 'Because death – no different to life – is natural; there is nothing special to say about it.'¹⁰⁹

Now, if a Chinese scholar, having this body of thought, were to stand before the *Little girl with dead bird*, how would he observe it – as someone, moreover, living in the twenty-first century? The picture is a Western work of art. It shows a girl with a dead bird in her hands, looking earnestly into the distance. In the Chinese tradition, a picture, as a phenomenon, is part of a process of depiction, itself part of modulating, regulating the appearance of the world.¹¹⁰ The Western work of art is indebted to an entirely different concept of genesis and of participation in the world. According to Chinese thinking, a picture obtains in its processual nature showing through, in those processes which have given and continue to give rise to it as a phenomenon. Thus, for example, brush, tusche, silk, and paper were traditionally preferred as materials, anything making something hard is avoided, in distinction to the Brussels portrait composed of wood that is hard and oil colour that is opaque. That portrait shows two figures in front of an abstract background. Over the course of the eighth and ninth centuries, according to our Western calendar, landscape painting drove back the older, direct portrayal of figures in the art of portraiture in China, for landscapes were assigned greater subtlety with participating in depicting what happens in the world. In that participation figures are only hinted at, coming and going prevails, and Nature stretches in nuanced and finely distinguished variations across scroll pictures, which did not permanently hang in the space but – like a book for reading – were spread out for observing them instead. In its form today, moreover, the *Little girl with dead bird* appears to be an allegory of life and death. One theme is brought to light, directly expressed. As already with the art of portraiture, such a creative approach is experienced as being not very subtle – and, as a result, held less in esteem, in the way artistic depictions are understood inside processes of worldly phenomena. The portrait would not be experienced in regard of an *exterior*, an *outside*, as the gaze portrayed might suggest in the Western context, for every distance is seen as part of the same worldly process, and in that process even death and life constitute only one of the regulating polarities, with which the cosmic course of the world, the *tao*, incessantly takes shape. In that regard, the allegorical way of seeing once again presents itself as being thoroughly Western.[111] In the thinking of immanence it is always about finding the way *into* the regulatory activity of taking shape, not about taking on a different plane. The allegorical way of seeing observes what is portrayed as standing in for something general, while the immanent way of proceeding attempts to illuminate, by varying situational contexts and following allusions in accordance with their efficacy.[112] In this way, concretely going in always denotes a going along, an accompanying in the change of what is experienced and of our own experience with that.

The *Little girl with dead bird* is an *old* work of art, and as such it is difficult to be able to observe it only against the backdrop of modern painting, the way it dominates in the global art market as well as in China, borrowing the Western view. The alien experience of an old European work of art reflects the question as to *old* particular ways of observing (playing here for a moment with the 'perspectives of interpretation', which Jullien speaks of[113]). At first glance, the Brussels portrait would be – in the very removed sense – only comparable to a genre that was not highly regarded in

China traditionally, since it did not evoke the picture's participatory nature in the conditions for its appearance very much. The gaze of the little girl as well as the contrast of life and death would not be interpreted in regard of an *outside* but, rather, observed in regard of immanent possibilities in the directness of its portrayal, in varying the ways of seeing, in what is concrete in the world. In doing so, the gaze – even if inner collecting was always preferred later on, in view of landscape painting – would not be insignificant. Before the rise of landscape painting, according to Jullien, it was said that for portrait artists 'according to a famous formula, which also became an adage among painters, the capacity to render the spirit of an individual' supposedly depends upon another capacity entirely, namely, 'to orient [the] eyes and, secondarily, in the contour of the cheeks and the cheekbones'.[114] Not the mouth and the eyes, as often is the case in European painting, but instead the cheeks and the eyes are seen together here, above all else. The cheeks of the little girl are no longer the chubby cheeks of an infant but are nevertheless childlike in their shape (the reddening may be part of a reworking). The earnest mouth, therefore, would be captured in the childlike cheeks, with the gaze into the distance. The childlike nature of the cheeks carries the gaze, too. Yet how was it interpreted? In contrast to the hands, to the bird?

Death is not anything outrageous in Ancient China but, rather, part of a natural immanence. The violent death of the bird would speak of 'disorder', 'violence'; it would be an indication, a clue, an allusion that could be varied. 'Violence' belongs to those things 'the master "does not speak"' about – the 'master' being Confucius – because it does not lead to regulation but to deregulation instead, far from natural re-creation.[115] The ethical violation against this re-creation makes at the same time a moral authority out of the latter, such that ethics and the observation of Nature constitute two poles of one way of seeing. Might the bird be only a symbol, one for the offence against modulation, against the re-creation of the natural course of things?[116] It was not devoured by a cat or taken by hunters as a catch;

after it was killed, there was nothing more than that, stagnation, death absent any reconnection to what happens further. Is there any comparable portrayal in Ancient China? The picture shows what can happen but contributes nothing to the course of the world. Is it in that way that the picture is opposite something alienating? That an old picture shows something that repeating what the Ancients had to say does not help? And in that case what would comprise access to the world in showing it after all? The little girl, too, is stagnant, abiding. She could be described as 'full of cares', right there where 'the flow stagnates'. In that way we would emphasise the nature of the 'moment', of the 'transition' in which she finds herself. Like the bird, she is part of the natural world, and the virtue of humaneness obliges her even to a kind of solidarity with it – she did become more human thanks to the bird, after all; in dealing with it, and in doing right by it, she could evolve as well.[117] The little girl will again be able to find the way into the flow of life, overcome stagnation, grow as a result of it, grow in this leave-taking that first made her aware of, made her able to experience this coming and going. In this way, then, does the picture lose its 'horror'? In any event, the dark background would no longer suggest that, would at most only function as fund, as source, in the polarity of the invisible background and the visible appearance, figuration. And the gaze into the distance would not pertain to anything existentially imponderable. That is not the case; the little girl is just looking upward. She abides, poses no question, only opens up her gaze, though not to the observer, not to anything opposite her. She looks into the distance, almost impassively, inertly on the inside, in the *in-between* of what? In the transition of coming and going, still before any dealing with it, with that first experience that makes her abide.

Thoughts on life and death (II)

'The universe we can survey, that is to say, what is within the optical horizon, has a depth of approximately ten billion light years,' Lars Gustafsson has remarked.[118] With the naked eye we can recognise the stars in it at a distance of up to ten light years; these form our 'starry heaven'. Our galaxy accommodates hundreds of billions of stars, with a diameter of a 100,000 light years. The Andromeda Nebula, the nearest galaxy, is two million light years distant. '50 million light years farther is a formation our local portion belongs to, which comprises more than 500,000 galaxies.'[119] What does that tell us?

Approximately four billion years ago – not light years! – the conditions for life on our planet began to develop. Organic life as such has been in effect for five hundred million years.

Being conscious of death, which is part of life, is one of the possible conditions for being human: It was with humanity that archaeologically documented burial rituals first arose. Other animals may know grief – like primates, for instance – yet only Homo sapiens (and the Neanderthal) buried their deceased with the trappings of ritual. Why?

In Jochen Rack's written accounts on death, I read: '(...) *died peacefully in his sleep*, as they say, is not how the dead man looked, but instead gruesomely distorted and wrenched from his dying, like after a struggle. I understood that in the history of humanity, death had been experienced for a long time as something that befalls you by force, from the outside (...).'[120]

When Hans Blumenberg remarks that the fundamental situation of humanity is not to know what we are doing and *nevertheless having to act*, then death is the manifestation of unknowing par excellence, the challenge only to act, set loose from its influence, to find ourselves still in symbolic practices.

Unknowing is radical only in mystical traditions or in philosophical positions from Antiquity (Socrates) or, as the case may be, since the Enlightenment (Hume). In a world of inclusive gods or of one exclusive God, the *outside* that Rack is talking about was associated with more and more divine influence, as a partial shared knowing or a revelation.

The *source*, the *fund* of immanence – invulnerable Nature, *Heaven* – bears witness to a trust in the world that is at risk of being lost not only in the expanse of astronomical calculations – we are inclined to recall, like Gustafsson, the saying of Blaise Pascal that 'engulfed in the infinite immensity of spaces whereof I know nothing, and which know nothing of me, I am terrified'[121] – but also in the scope of the Industrial Revolution and globalisation, with their consequences for species death and with the distortions, disruptions of natural processes of regeneration extending to the violation of the biosphere.

If death is a question of life, is any gaze above and beyond Nature – as understood today – really needed? Furthermore, would Nature not be the horizon for this question?

* * *

The *outside* of death, above and beyond humanity and Nature, unfolds into the religious, as a belief in gods. Jan Assmann described at length the principle of prehistoric worlds of gods, which functioned as unifying principle and balance of power for cosmos, humanity, and society, providing meaning and order. The *unity* of cosmos, humanity, and society manifested itself as a synergy – via many forces, many gods – and yet all of them served this *unifying* principle. The gods had 'withdrawn', perhaps, yet they *remained part of this world*.

This *outside* becomes radicalised with the distinction made in one God who rules out any and all synergy, who stands as the exclusive principle on the *other side* of the forces of Nature, is not associated with them, is proven in supernatural miracles, as being *not of this world*. This exclusivity of God creates an absolute claim, expressed in the either/or, in truly living his grace, and in the falseness of *this world*. As Assmann remarks, 'a "hermeneutics of difference" takes' the place of synergy and 'translation'.[122] And this first positing of difference, as the initial instance of its founding, is what so-called monotheism has in common with later philosophy.[123] For whereas in the one case distinguishing between true and false religion was made for the first time, in the other case the distinction between true and false knowledge was first differentiated. As an Egyptologist, Assmann writes in detail: 'This distinction, articulated (...) in the principles of identity, noncontradiction, and the excluded middle (*tertium non datur*), is commonly associated with the name of Parmenides, who lived in the sixth century BCE (...). The new concept of knowledge introduced by the Greeks is no less revolutionary in nature than the new concept of religion introduced by the Jews (...). Both concepts are characterized by an unprecedented drive to differentiation, negation, and exclusion. Ever since there has been science, and with it a knowledge, based on the distinction between true and false cognition, that distinguishes itself from error and opens itself to criticism through its manner of reasoning, there have also been such distinctions as those between *muthos* and *logos* (...), which correspond precisely to the distinction between pagan idolatry and religion.'[124] From that point forwards, there has therefore been the distinction between 'non-scientific knowledge' and 'scientific knowledge' as well as that between correct and false 'scientific knowledge'. In this way, 'belief' and 'knowledge' enter into a conflict in which belief raises its profile and gains visibility precisely as a result of considering the counter-evidential to be true (à la Tertullian, in the sense of the motto: *credo quia absurdum*). In this case, characterised by the same logic, belief in God and philosophy stand side by side when they both distance themselves from magic, superstition, idolatry, and other forms of 'false' religion and 'unknowing-ness' – to the benefit of a conflict between theology and ontology, a tension that will usher in medieval scholasticism, and which will not clear until the Enlightenment.

For understanding death and life, death thus leads for the first time *out of this world*, and the scientific exploration of death will not make it any clearer but subsequently only identify the cause of death ('heart failure'). Attesting to its naturalness through science, through the break with nature, appears inverted. Jochen Rack writes: 'In medical terms, my grandfather died from organ failure as a result of complications from cancer, and the doctor, who was called after grandfather died, checked the box with the term *"natural"* as the cause of death on the death certificate.'[125] In this situation, we no longer find ourselves in the *fund* of immanence – to which death belongs as naturally as life – but, rather, housed in a scientific world, based on difference and analysis.

* * *

This appears to be the situation in which death confronts us today: as a cause, from *outside*. Can we understand the portrait *Little girl with dead bird* in this way? Which *outside* do animals know? It is a sign of exclusive religions that their God only turns to human beings, as the lord of lords over his creations. The association of cosmic zodiac signs and 'holy animals' is rejected theologically as much as it is discredited scientifically. The 'animal world' is as re-*miss* in the natural sciences as 'Heaven' is in astronomy.

The cause of the little bird's death does not matter. The gaze of the little girl looking upwards does not arise from any observation, consideration, or insight. She does not experience the world from a distance. She is affected by something *that she does not yet understand*. 'It is only a sparrow.'

The scientific/matter-of-fact gaze cannot satisfy the child. For she is confused, and does not wonder, for instance, about the 'magical world of Nature', as a first instance of interest in the natural sciences. Wonder would have pertained to the hopping, dancing, flying sparrow. Dead, it escapes observation. And science does not open up any other gaze – whether in childlike wonder or from an adult distance. As *theoria*, observation, it would only be about the observation *as such* – yet never about a little girl with an ordinary, dead bird in her hands, the way it is in art. The picture appears untimely. And I remember only too well a talk with a chemistry teacher – after my explanations for her and her students before the portrait, as to why it was even hanging here at all, in the Old Masters collection. It was obviously not the motif that could be so convincing in her eyes – rather, in the end it was the fact that the portrayal with the dead bird had to do with a singular portrait of a child in Flemish art. It was as a piece of evidence, 'Exhibit A', that it apparently earned its place.

* * *

The motivating force of belief does not become evident from mere negation, as Nietzsche alleged. Even though Sigmund Freud underscored the psychic 'power of sublimation' in counter-evidential testimonies, there still remained – even in Nietzsche's case already – 'feelings of listlessness' that urge belief, to the greatest extent, in fact, when reality ought to be negated, overcome – the *vale of tears*. Assmann casts doubt on this: 'Nietzsche denounced the principles of salvational justice as "slave morality". He, too, believed them to be an invention of biblical monotheism, which he therefore regarded as the religion of the downtrodden and underprivileged, born of the rensentment they felt towards the victorious Greco-Roman culture, which represented the "superior" values of nobility, wealth, strength and beauty. No one less an eminence than Max Weber vehemently supported him in this. Whoever is able to show that the biblical principles of redemptive justice are also to be found in the wisdom traditions of ancient Near Eastern cultures, and that they formed a widespread basis for regulating the lives of individuals, communities and states, would clear biblical monotheism of this charge, and could further demonstrate that these principles are completely unrelated to resentment and slave morality.'[126] As an Egyptologist, Assmann instead draws attention to the distinguishing power of 'secondary religions', that is, those that make the distinction between inclusivity and exclucity of belief and, in this sense, challenge us to a *decision*, demand a *confession* that attests to the conviction of the individual in the community arising with that belief, as a vow of fidelity between humanity and God. In this context, Theo Sundermeier spoke of the 'invention of the inner self', as a person making conscientious decisions who is oriented towards the human confession of faith and the revelation of God, towards mutual scripturality, obligation, towards *covenant*.

Aligning a lifestyle towards true and false, this 'invention of the inner self' drew its strength from the non-visible. The explication of natural evidence likewise denotes: making visible. The explication of natural evidence fails, for instance, on account of the phenomenon of love. It is the strange world of Christian thought in which *love* is attested to *by* distinguishing into true and false. This is likewise natural evidence: *that* there is love, true love, that is. But the explication fails. Is this where the case arises in Western thought, in which the *power* and *logic of expression* are not of further help, where *dealing with* things leads only to *praxis*, to practices, actions, signs, gestures? Is this what Christianity has an *answer* for, unsatisfactory or not? For if love is seen as a *human* phenomenon – that is, not just as individual fulfilment – then what form do we give this shared 'celebration'? Certainly not one of intimacy. And nevertheless one of a celebratory nature, of festivity. Perhaps ritual coming together goes hand in hand with these aporias. We may deny ourselves them, sticking to explications of what is evidential and of their impossibility in this case. Yet would that not be comparable to Wittgenstein's dictum that we must be silent about what we cannot speak about? And this concept narrows down explication, does it not? Does it recognise any thinking of what is indirect, thinking implicitly only what is effective? Does it deny poetry the right to speak, as 'fine verbiage'? From which standpoint does it issue this commandment?

Wittgenstein himself later said to his students: 'If you ask me whether or not I believe in a Judgement Day, in the sense in which religious people believe in it, I wouldn't say: "No. I don't believe there will be such a thing." It would seem to me utterly crazy to say this. And then I give an explanation: "I don't believe in ...", but then the religious person never believes what I describe. I can't say. I can't contradict that person.'[127]

Yet Ernst Tugendhat does contradict him: 'It is trivial that we cannot disprove the existence of a supernatural being any more than we can prove it, but that only means that the only thing that argues for it is the wish to do so, and consequently its existence is not disproved but, to be sure, the belief in that existence.'[128] Yet why should we 'wish' to believe in a God? Does not Tugendhat refer back to the question of need here, which would lead to resentment towards the 'natural evidence'? Or does he mean 'wish' in the Aristotelian sense, as ideal? Are ideals *wishful thinking*? I do not believe that Tugendhat is thinking along these lines. And he does not go as far as Nietzsche, either, whose position he describes as follows: 'There is no God, *and* that is also better for us (...).'[129] He describes his own mindset in a more nuanced way, and I would like to cite the crucial passage here again: 'I believe that the need for a belief in gods is not only a cultural but, rather, an anthropological phenomenon grounded in the structure of being human, on the one hand, but that it is impossible for humanity today to yield to this need, unless we deceive ourselves.'[130] With a view to the Chinese tradition, it remains to be seen whether the 'belief in gods' is anthropological. What, though, would alienate 'humanity today' from its anthropological 'structure'? This point, too, appears questionable to me. The question remains, then, whether we 'deceive' ourselves if we believe in a God. According to which criterion? In this regard, Tugendhat follows Bertrand Russell: according to the 'natural evidence'. Jan Assmann, too, sees the crux of the matter here: That is 'what revealed truth lacks'.[131] Its 'counter-evidential' strategy of what is efficacious in a radically invisible way *among human beings*, of the 'Pentecostal experience' of a 'Holy Spirit' – one of *their* coming together, in fact, as testimony of the covenant with God – these collective ways of acting in support of a celebration of the phenomenon of love, beyond the personal: These things appear only to be an answer to a dilemma – possibly anthropological – namely, the search for contact, for interaction where there is no insight that helps any longer, or as Blumenberg has described it: where symbolic forms, poetry, and rhetoric become the expression of that which eludes the direct grasp, visualisation, determinability. The 'natural evidence' is not *unambiguous* in that regard, for it can lead to phenomena that *exist*, but which are not accessible for any analytical utilisation, like the phenomenon of love. Philosophy, with its hermeneutics of difference, can describe it, but it cannot give any shape, any efficacy to it. A philosophical text does not make us 'fall in love'. The poetry of a situation, of a turn of phrase, of a glance, of a picture, of a sound, of a verse – all these moments in which love between individuals ignites, entangles, unfolds – they simply rule out analysing it, breaking it down, talking it out, pulling things apart. The human capacity for love – we do not need to exaggerate it religiously, but its collective contents rise not without having some shape. The

'Love Parades' and raves in pop culture prove that as much as religious festivities. Ultimately, the question is what perhaps argues for the religious exaggeration of love's collective contents. Can we speak seriously of the 'divine'?

Like Tugendhat, Ricœur was also concerned with a 'philosophical anthropology'.[132] And he likewise spoke of 'being bona fide', in spite of the French phrase 'honnête intellectuelle' – in his posthumous fragments even using the German 'Redlichkeit', as an allusion to Nietzsche, who 'denies Christians'[133] this honesty. At first he himself wonders whether he is 'following (...) the line of sacrificial theologies, of a death both offered for all people and destined to satisfy the implacable justice of a God who demands satisfaction from them for a sin itself worthy of death and who finds satisfaction in the "substitution" of the very Son of God the Father who dies in their place?'[134] It is precisely this line of thinking that Rudolf Boehm has described as the core of Christian belief. And as mentioned already in his fragment on Jacques Derrida, Ricœur also gives his account from this point of departure of 'what I do not believe. If "learning finally how to live" is to learn to die, to take into account absolute mortality without salvation, resurrection, or redemption, I share all the negative here. I too, I do not expect resurrection for myself (...).'[135] And in his historical reading of the Bible, he argues: '(...) the great antiquity of Abraham, the powerful scene of the crossing of the Red Sea, the wandering for forty days [sic] in the desert under the leadership of Moses, the conquest of Canaan (...); the story of Joseph, the glory of David. and the splendor of Solomon's temple, etc. (...) none of that actually happened, the archeological argument is unanswerable; not a trace of the passage, the occupation of the land, the building. *Nothing* historical before the 7th c., before Josiah (...). A small Judah taking over from a more powerful Israel/Samaria and setting off some fireworks before being swept aside in turn up to the deportation. The return follows, the time of Judaism and the new temple and theography under Persian influence. Here history runs into its bases; textual criticism and archeology go hand in hand.'[136]

Yet the historical evidence does not explain the motivations for the changes, as Aristotle had already argued when he characterised historiography as the portrayal of events, which did not follow any historical laws but, rather, human drives, anthropological dispositions, which the art of versification – tragedy, for instance – could illustrate in much more commensurate manner. Ricœur, too, thinks: '(...) devotion to a Name without an image (...). But what this [archaeological guide] will never explain.'[137] Why worship sheer textualisation, the formal reduction of what can be seen, the exclusive accentuation of the imaginary? 'Love' as an 'inner decision'? A question of conscience? Love 'for God'? The God who appears here feels faraway – faraway this belief in resurrection – Ricœur did not believe in that, either. The miracle of God becoming human, for lifting humanity in 'his glory' – it does not need repeating. Yet the 'kingdom of God' has not *come*, has not *come* to humankind. And with each season of Advent we can say: not yet. Still, the delay exceeds all human estimation, all our hope. Is that the 'weakness' of belief? For Ricœur it is much more a respect for those nameless dead, the crimes against humanity. After the horrors of annihilation, hoping 'for God' is irrelevant: '"the hope that she will survive me". All of the religious is there, as a link between my wanting to live and my own.'[138] For him, it is in that regard that hope plays out – between him and his affiliation with, his membership in collective forms of dealing with life and death, forms that know no determination, explanation, forms that compel our action, alone or with others. The religious components arise for him with 'the others', his community. In the process, he mistrusts what is 'immediate', 'fusional', 'intuitive', 'mystical' – with 'one exception, in the grace of a certain dying'.[139] It is this thought that leads him to the 'religious': that in dying a deeper connection from person to person might appear at times, if possible from individual to individual. He recalls Jorge Semprún, who accompanies the dying Maurice Halbwachs in the concentration camp at Buchenwald in 1944, and who realises that he cannot accompany this completely drained individual without saying a word, even if it is not a prayer. And so Semprún recites a few verses from Charles Baudelaire, '*O Death, old captain, it is time! let us lift anchor ...*', and he writes: 'His eyes brightened slightly, as though with astonishment. I continue to recite. When I reached the line ... *nos cœurs que tu connais sont remplis de rayons* [our hearts, which you know, are filled with light], a delicate tremor passed over the lips of Maurice Halbwachs.'[140] In another passage, the writer argues: 'Few "subjects" (...) can withstand the threat of death. This one brings into confrontation fraternity, death, that part of mankind which is today seeking to define itself as something far beyond the individual.'[141] As Ricœur comments, the individual who has to die alone becomes indistinguishable from one doomed to death. Ricœur continues: 'To be present at a death is more precise, more poignant than simply surviving. Taking part is a more pointlike test, more event-like. To survive is a long trajectory, at best that of mourning (...).'[142] To rejoin that look is a final *outside*, for anyone who looks. Every individuality is communicated in this *outside for one another*, into its own groundlessness, *for one another* – that is the brightening in the gaze that Semprún speaks of. The *outside for one another* opens up the relationship of Self and Other. Ricœur clings to this opening without saying what it opens on. It is the residue of his belief.

Interpreting this opening as religious would mean seeing it in regard of another Third Party. This may still appear possible, even if only subliminal, to those practising a hermeneutics of difference – and I use the term here in all its multi-layered nature, attested to, for instance, by Ricœur's historical treatise *Memory, History, Forgetting*.[143] For the phenomenologist Ricœur, this *outside for one another* would mean a kind of bilateralness, which springs from a contrast, from a shifting of gazes. Through this shift, the gazes each supposedly also see, also 'appresent' that which eludes the *closer look*, the grounds for my recognising, my inspecting as made manifest in shapes. These grounds, this source, this *fund* does not exist as such – as an accompanying phenomenon only, it conveys the looking, on the margins. In this way, however, it is given the potential to see these forms come to the fore. In the gaze of the Other we become conscious of the passing nature of this interest, and yet it reveals itself not primarily in its manifestation – facial features, the position of the eyes – but instead as a whole. In this case that can only mean: not as a casing, a shell, not as a 'looking past' but, rather, as an obvious contrast to which the sources, the fund – the glimmer in the eyes of the Other – first imparts its communicating look, its gaze that becomes recognisable by figures of seeing (changes in a glance, facial expressions). The fund is the immemorial openness of this seeing.

Bernhard Waldenfels describes, for instance, how an opening to another potential Third Party with this contrast is indeed indirectly effective, yet always only as a mental image, a notion, a construction, as the plane for giving shape, making understood, being related to language. In that regard, his fundamental thought is how, as a process, *eluding* specifically provokes the desire to be able to address it, as well as how the search for any possible interaction can only ever come back to the desire for this interaction, never to the process of eluding itself. If we say 'time passes', then this passing awakens in me the demand for being able to find a way to deal with it. Yet I cannot address time ticking away itself but, rather, my demand for dealing with it – by giving expression to the desire, through language, vis-à-vis others, or even in the form of an object, by making a photo, putting an album together, visualising: 'That has occurred.' The same is true for the Other opposite me – I similarly cannot grasp the Other as such, facets of him always elude me, though in his regard I can sense the desire for finding interaction with him, a way of dealing that refers back to this desire, and yet is only possible this way. That means, as Waldenfels says: '*I myself begin, though never with me, but somewhere else instead* (...).'[144] My doings stem from a desire that begins with provocation, which always only becomes perceptible belatedly, namely, when the eluding has set in. As a temporal process, it circumvents spatial resistance, which I am able to *oppose* – it is an *experience I am faced with*, one that unnoticeably sets in, becomes perceptible, like forgetting.

I cannot directly influence forgetting, only indirectly: by finding memory aids, some form in which I can store something, images from memory, words of transmissibility, from one situation to the next. Here is where construction begins, out of the aptitude for language. This construction is, for example, the determination of a standpoint of our own, in terms of a relationship. François Jullien, for instance, recalls the founding of these kinds of relationships in Aristotelian *physics*: '(...) in order to think of Nature, the physicist has to think motion (*kinesis*), which is the principle of Nature; and to think of motion, he has to think – in accordance with the place where the change of place occurs – the time that serves to measure it'.[145] And whoever thinks of time as the medium of motion will also have to think of some form of immobility, by which it is 'ignited'. In this way, Aristotelian physics leads to the question of ontology and theology: immobility or eternity.

Instead of thinking relational motion – through which the problem of time and eternity, for instance, is even posed in the first place – Jullien recommends returning to the notion of continual change, as it was developed traditionally in China. Waldenfels, rather, opens up the possibility of an indirect 'as-well-as': The question of time informs his fundamental notion of eluding. Time thus appears initially as a phenomenon of delayed experience. This experience asks for interaction – only in regressing towards experience can that interaction attest, furthermore, to what provoked it, the phenomenon of time. We can only speak out of our desire for a response to time, even if we cannot directly answer its eluding us. The answer will therefore have to satisfy the desire for it without being able to do so conclusively, for neither desire nor answer together constitute a circle that can be closed but were, rather, compelled into a contrast with one another from the motion of eluding. Eluding takes effect behind our own desire. We can try to shield, to protect what is behind this desire, in constructing 'naturalness', 'cyclical systems', 'system immanence'. The cultivation of a 'lifeworld' aims at that at times. However, the anthropological dimension is revealed in what is inconclusive, what cannot be regulated, in what determines and constitutes us. And that is what we try to escape from birth up to death. This search for 'self-determination' is thoroughly necessary, anthropologically speaking – after all, we come into this world without any hide or claws, naked, in need of protection. The constructing begins to come to a close – since the desire always remains vulnerable – where the answer, form, creation is further developed to the level of *autonomy*, as started in geometry, which allows us to design space to be three-dimensional and, in this way, understands the line as well as the point to be the precondition of space. In this way Aristotelian 'time', for instance, is just as modeled on 'space' as the Platonic dialectic is on the triangle – with the base between the reversible points of the Self and the Other, and the apex of their common comparability, the position of the Third Party. Inasmuch as this kind of physical, ontological, theological, or dialectical thinking avoids regressing towards experience, it constructs to the same extent norms of modeled evidence as well as counter-evidential acts related to it. That has been the phenomenological critique of this process ever since Edmund Husserl wrote *Die Krisis der europäischen Wissenschaften und die transzendentale Phänomenologie* in 1936.[146]

In the work of Waldenfels, therefore, an intermediate position would become clear: It exists in the indirect effect of the paradigmatic figure-ground contrast of experience upon 'representative', 'formative' imagining and thinking. When Ricœur describes the gaze between a dying person and the individual attending him as a 'residue of his belief', the question of the gaze leads at the same time into the phenomenological realm. This allows for a 'hermeneutics of difference', yet only as a response, as an answer *of our own* to what is experienced. And the latitude afforded this particular answer is as situationally bound as it is contingent, as an inconclusive, non-predetermined space of also spontaneous, coincidental, excessive findings. How we interpret being singularly affected, how we note the gaze, is decided within the horizon of our own possibilities for findings, with which the desire for expressing it can be given voice, in the saying – with the aid of the possibilities understood through language – in what can be said, in what is said. Though a religious experience can be handed down in canonical speech, it cannot be vividly shared, only in the attempt *itself* to speak of it, out of our being affected ourselves. It is in this sense that the hermeneutical religious philosopher Ingolf Dalferth, for instance, places the emphasis on concrete speech and thought, when he writes: 'God is entirely different *to what is said of God somewhere or thought about God somewhere else.*'[147] Such 'concrete negation', as Waldenfels notes, 'is consistent with motifs of excess and deprivation, whereas total Otherness merely reverses the dialectic of totality'.[148] This 'concrete negation' frees religiosity from solely dialectic alternation – and thus also from the compulsion of its affirmative reversal. The experience of the gaze, which Ricœur writes about, is ambiguous. According to Waldenfels, this ambiguity is always to be taken as the point of departure phenomenologically; no premise can be 'insinuated' to it. Thus, for instance, he writes: 'Whoever insinuates in advance something or someone – a conveyor, and initiator, or even a partner – to the experience we are faced with skips over the vivid experience and interrupts it before it is given voice. (...) Let us assume that the religious springs from an originary experience and does not represent any mere biological, psychological, political, economic, or imaginary epiphenomenon. (...) The excessive and alien nature of the religious experiences we are faced with would be lost, if we wanted to define them in advance as religious or God-given. Strictly speaking, therefore, there are no religious phenomena or religious experiences; there is only being affected and being spoken to, which is proven – or not proven – *as religious, as divine* in the answer of the religious person, of the believer. the widespread projection theories [note: on the idea that religious belief is supposedly wishful thinking, cf. the position of Tugendhat] put the cart before the horse by relocating the retroactive 'If' to the prior pathos (...)',[149] in other words, to being affected as passively incurred.

How do we interpret experiences that cannot be reduced to corporeality, which exceeds what is individual and yet cannot be explained politically, within the community; which we cannot cope with by strategies of economy and conduct; and which are not figments of the imagination we can drive away? Experiences in which our own conditionality appears, shared experiences, human ones like those of our own connectedness, as Semprún describes them, for instance? When we first-hand, of our own, in our singularity become conscious of the groundless exemplary nature of precisely this singularity? Comparable, for instance, to how parents become conscious of the exemplary nature of life through their own children, of their own exemplary nature for their own parents? This experience is human. Poetry speaks of it without making a religion or 'projection theory' out of it, without putting the cart before the horse. At the same time, indicating and interpreting go hand in hand, something is indicated and we indicate it, just like saying also only appears in what is said, experiencing in what is experienced. We cannot separate indicating from interpreting. What, then, does the latter mean?

Whereas theology takes the testimony of God as its point of departure, the philosophy of religion, in contrast, treats the conditions of this testimony, the potentials of the religious. In doing so, the central question is how – or whether – Nature and meaning relate to one another.[150] Nature arose – cosmologically, physically, chemically, biologically – and is vulnerable. Just as death arose with life, with the Neanderthal and Homo sapiens there ultimately also arose a way of dealing with it, in rituals, myths, practices, religions. Does Nature matter to humankind equally – or is it indifferent as opposed to humanity? Both. What does 'meaning' mean in this context? A difference vis-à-vis what is doubly indifferent, that is, in regard of *being indifferent* and of mattering equally. Precisely this circumstance is connected, for example, in the 'notion of God' for Judaism and Christianity as well as for Islam: its indifferent nature vis-à-vis humanity, its mattering equally as opposed to humanity and the distinct nature of every human being, in the 'omnipotence of God', in his 'justice' and/or 'love', and in the 'judgement' and/or 'gaze' for every individual. In this way, 'God' becomes a catch-all term for the connective efficacy of human difference in the indifference of Nature, as the inclusion of Nature and humankind in distinction to one another. At the same time, this grounds 'his' exteriority.

Have we outgrown this central question concerning how, and/or whether, Nature and meaning are interrelated? This is decisive in the interpretation attempts of the religious and/or of their defensive criticism. In this case, too, the question is *how* we think. Whoever thinks, like Aristotle, of motion in terms of a point – of a cause that aims at an effect in reaching a second point – can scientifically take a Big Bang as the point of departure, or metaphysically consider it to be an 'unmoved mover', or theologically even a 'creator'; the thinking always remains within a teleology, a thinking from A to B, cause and effect, causality. According to Waldenfels, this sort of differentiation cannot be thought. Later, I will go into how that is so. At this juncture, suffice it to say that even the *epoché* of phenomenology – the reduction to phenomena, as with the gaze, for example, implies latitude as well as limits for interpretation. Waldenfels does not deny himself assumptions of religious experience. The differentiation in claiming to put a 'creator' first, however, contradicts its logical premises, as I will demonstrate presently.

In this regard, Waldenfels' position is distinct from that of Levinas or Ricœur.[151] Whereas Ricœur and Levinas philosophise with Protestantism and Judaism in the background – that is to say, that there are moments in which the undeniable nature of their search for belief becomes clear, in pivot points that also determine their intuition and motivation – this aspect is lacking in Waldenfels. He remains much more indebted to Husserl's factual conscientiousness and writes in fundamental terms: 'A philosophy of religion, understood as a phenomenology of religion, is neither religious nor irreligious. It cannot do any more than defend misinterpretations and give voice to the phenomena, without having the last word.'[152]

In the question of the gaze – of especial importance for Ricœur, Waldenfels, or even Levinas – there are therefore overlaps between phenomenologically and religiously loaded thinking. Phenomenologically speaking, there are moreover overlaps with what Jullien has described as traditional Chinese thought: Waldenfels thinks from the aspect of *going* – the process of withdrawing, eluding – and this supposedly leads to an *experience*, which appears as a *contrast*, a contrast of desiring, demanding, and of connoting, denoting, noting. The mental figuration of contrast is based on the shifting of *fund* – of source – and form, of the simultaneous separation of both, of their bilateralness.

At the same time, there are striking differences between the responsive thinking of the phenomenologist and that of traditional Taoism. The first difference concerns the *fund* of Nature and thus its *immanence*. Waldenfels, too, affirmatively cites Pascal: '"Le silence éternel de ces espaces infinis m'effraie." (*Pensée* 201/206: 'The eternal silence of these infinite spaces alarms me.') Casting me back on myself, this silence grows out of the indifference of a Nature devoid of and distant from humanity, which I do not know, and which does not know me (*Pensée* 68/205). This indifference impresses us as more alien than any enemy could.'[153] According to Ancient Chinese thought, however, Nature is not '*alien*' but, rather, "appealing" (...)'.[154] The latter we would have to affirm, agreeing as does Waldenfels: The responsivity is effected precisely from the 'appeal' of things and persons. Thus, in his foundational text *Bruchlinien der Erfahrung* ('Fault lines of experience'), Waldenfels writes: 'The fact that things make an appeal (...) to us can also mean that forces particular (...) to nature are released, which go beyond any pragmatic and technical use for things, and which take part in experiences we face without any input from us. At the same time, these pre-figurative experiences are the breeding ground for creating reality in an artistic, mythological/religious, and thinking manner, one exceeding the context of normal experience. Even the asceticism of scientific research, which refrains from being immediately relevant to life, allows things their own significance (...).'¹⁵⁵ In his opinion, though, the appealing character of Nature does not rule out its 'hostility'.¹⁵⁶ For what guarantees its inexhaustible immanence, the 'way'? Even if the physical evidence is also 'modeled', corresponds to models that come about by *disregarding* experience – no photo has been made from space with the naked eye but, rather, 'blindly', according to calculations (no different to a pilot flying at night) – that still does not mean that they do not have to be proven in reality, in other words, in the resistance of matter. And at this juncture, we would recall the quote from Lars Gustafsson: that the earth appears by all estimates to be an infinitesimally small exception in a universe that, in what is accessible to us until now, knows no other life. Nature appears to be a happy coincidence, an extreme exception to an oxygen-free rule that is hostile to life. The atmosphere has the effect of being immanent, like a constantly regenerating casing, a shell. And the significance of water in Taoist thought seems to point precisely to that, as Jullien emphasises: 'There is nothing, though, that is more difficult to untangle, in its passage and in its nature, than *water*. It is, (Wang Fuzhi) (...) notes, in its most subtle form – as barely condensed, inscrutable precipitate – distributed everywhere in the atmosphere. At the same time, in its most comprehensive form it appears in riverways and oceans that cannot be traversed. It has a share in both: in that which, like the earth, has (...) already assumed form; and in that which, like the air, is still completely in motion.'¹⁵⁷ Water, too, can be 'dangerous', as Jullien remarks, though it is not stylised as 'hostility', as 'counterclaim'.

Then again, Waldenfels likes to quote Nietzsche as saying: 'Man is the "not yet fixed animal" (...).'¹⁵⁸ Waldenfels has commented on him repeatedly in his work. Thus, for instance, he writes in *Der Stachel des Fremden* ('The Sting of the alien'), 'The situation of the "not yet fixed animal" corresponds to an *open, unready world* (see Husserl VI, 180) (...).'¹⁵⁹ The 'unready' contradicts a 'totality'. Or: 'As a not yet fixed animal he is compelled to reduce and select possibilities (...). He is compelled to invent, to organise, by which he enforces an order upon things, his body, and himself in connection with Others.'[160] Here, this 'enforcing', this violent intervention, is already understood anthropologically. *Activity* springs from an Ancient Greek correspondence to passivity, which is not indicated in Classical Chinese, but which Waldenfels also does not want to give the last word, without ruling passivity out as a result. Thus, the desire as *passio* constitutes for him an intermediate moment of passivity in eluding and of activity in responding – whether this happens verbally, gesturally or palpably, manually, in the *intervening*.

Similarly, he considers the concept 'element' to be an intermediate moment of, traditionally speaking, passively thought matter and actively manifested form. In this way, he goes *between these opposites*, respectively, in order to release them in their binarity, to the benefit of a dynamic, processual differentiation. So doing, he escapes renewed polarisation, just as Jullien also carries out when he challenges Western thinking on time tout court in order to argue, on the contrary, on the basis of Classical Chinese thinking on continual change.[161] Yet the Sinologist and philosopher Jullien does not go much further than to make a possible introduction of this thinking into the Western context, in spite of his own claim to be determining these Western origins anew. He indicates points of contact for specific, local experiences of Nature and life, too, though always directed towards the newly chosen pole, the Taoist way of thinking. Elucidating what is our own based on the alien is one way of proceeding. What, though, are the consequences for what is our own? In Jullien's writing, we find the gaps to Western thinking bridged only in places, as estimations. Only in isolated instances do we find a 'phenomenology of the moment', for example, which he speaks of at the beginning of his essay *Vital nourishment*.[162] And until now his thinking of the immediate, which he associates with this phenomenology as well as how it supposedly '*trans*-appears' in metaphor, remains without further elaboration, only a prospect.[163]

This talk of the 'not yet fixed animal' is to say that humanity has supposedly not fully fit into Nature and not fully adapted to any biotope. It is thinking beyond the evolutionary character of change, towards a break that distinguishes humans from animals. This break reportedly allows rule-breaking in the first place, between nature and culture, culture and civilisation, city and virtuality. 'What becomes problematic', Waldenfels continues, 'is the functionalising and normalising, when the excess of what is unequal is forgotten or repressed. What is not yet fixed in the human animal would be compensated for through artificial fixations, identifications.'[164]

The 'excess of what is unequal' refers to the aforementioned process of differentiation. According to Waldenfels, this process is not owing to any immanence but, rather, is manifested fundamentally in two instances: a) an originary indirectness in the effect of that differentiation, b) the abrupt arising of bilateralness as a contrast phenomenon. So, for example, he mentions that we ought to remember how 'own' and 'alien' would emerge bilaterally from *differentiating* as responsive basic terms: 'As in the case of "I" and "You", it entails a contrast phenomenon in which both contrast values are formed into one. (...) In the beginning, there is *not unity but, rather, difference.*'[165]

Here, difference can be understood in a two-fold way: in the dialectical based first on the Self, next as the negation of that Self. Yet what effects the shift in symmetry? To what extent does geometric abstraction respond to a desire for its autonomy, issuing from the eluding, from the pathos of passivity? And which status does the concept of difference have in this expanding notion?

Eluding cannot be conceived as something, as an entity; it is revealed only in the effects that accompany it, which we can experience and/or make comprehensible. The phenomenologist Waldenfels believes: 'I am not the originator of time, nor does time affect me as something that befalls me from outside; the current distinction of activity and passivity fails here.'[166] The effect of time is not outside me – and, for instance, in this sense indirect (since I cannot directly bring about time). Rather, it is radically indirect inasmuch as it brings about my desire. The very temporality, then, of every denotation – of denominating in the sign of something – is opposed to an identity with the selfsame, to the extent it can in turn be postulated (circularly). In accordance with its denoting, every denotation is cleft, shunted into itself, just as everything said is in accordance with the saying, everything seen with seeing.

Accordingly, these shifts are not negations of a positive thing. It is by them that *contrasts* of complements are ignited. Since these are not attained negatively (in accordance, for instance, with a negative dialectic, like that of Sartre or Adorno), then their bilateralness is not identical with their selfsameness. *This* difference would be a much more *responsively genealogical* difference.

Waldenfels connotes this difference by the figure of the chiasma. In this regard, there are three ways of interpretation: According to Paul Valéry, the first means a crisscrossing of two gazes, 'akin to the crossing over of the optic nerves (...)'.[167] The second form is this latter optical intersection. The *responsive* difference, however, does not arise *from* two phenomena – in the way two gazes cross one another, or two eyes generate a visual impression. It is, rather, an *intertwining*, which leads in the first place to binary phenomena and, doing so, does not itself correspond to any binary scheme. That is where the distinction to the first two variations lies.

Eluding arouses a desire for an answer – an answer that can only address the desire for it, one which never reaches the state of being affected. The opposite of pathic passivity and intentional activity becomes possible thanks to *passio*, which simultaneously breaks down, expands, stretches the opposite, as the contrasting moment that leads to the aforementioned bilateralness. Bilateral, and not alternating, because the opposite is grounded in, is configured for the shift and cannot be turned around. In this way, *passio* enables a juxtaposition that never leads to the direct encounter. In this sense, what connects the third figure of the chiasma is the bilateral, irreversible, irresolvable contrast. The point is that this radical form of chiasma – intertwining – does not exclude the synthetic form but, rather, motivates it. There is a connection between chiasma as intertwining and the second form – the crossing over of what is to be seen *into a visual impression* – and it is comparable to the connection from pathos to the logos of sensuality, to the synthecised image.

In its experience, then, the 'not yet fixed animal' would be cleft, shunted into itself, 'temporally displaced', dynamic, and dependent on constants, which it always also has to establish, even if only as *an image that we make for ourselves*. The appeal of Nature always conveys an 'excess of possibilities', as Waldenfels writes with a view to possible kinds of order, constants, constructions. That is to say 'that he is obliged to make determinations, to commit to a certain "how", to a "this way and no other"'.[168] He describes the latitude found within these commitments in terms of four possible notions of order: the *responsive* kind on the *threshold* of ordinary and extra-ordinary; the *teleological* kind regarding our own striving; the *normative* type regarding obligations and intentions; as well as the *selective* one, which takes as its point of departure an *excess of possibilities*, those we seek to capture partially, poetically.[169] The last one appears to be most comparable to Taoist thinking. For in it what is moral is, again, composed situationally and *not* normatively. On top of that, change is not conceived of as motion from A to B, as the striving towards a goal (telos) by which the way is determined – in the manner that the established form determines the process of Becoming, as Being. And the immanence of Nature has no exteriority, no *outside* of what is regulating, regenerating.

The concept '*threshold*' sounds softer, less dramatic than that of a break. It applies to the phenomenon of eluding, which is not abrupt or momentary, as a break or a rupture might suggest. Nevertheless, it involves a quality, an aspect of differentiation that cannot be regulated. It entails a 'excessive claim' ('Überanspruch'), as Waldenfels says, that can have an *occupying* effect, as an excessive demand resulting from the situation. Experiencing death as slipping, slipping away, eluding, passing away is certainly one such excessive demand.

In the notes from his *Philosophischen Tagebuch* ('Philosophical diary'), Waldenfels remarks in this context: 'On Blumenberg's *Work on myth*, p. 21: Anthropogenesis means replacing a "habitual adaptive system of challenge and performance". I understand that this way: humanity as a "not yet fixed animal". This state of *not being adapted* points in two directions: towards a reality, on the one hand, that surprises, overpowers, threatens us, that intertwines our wishes and designs – and towards our aspirations and intentions, on the other hand, that press beyond the given reality: the potential for wishes and fantasies. Two-fold excess, in other words, like an arsenal of questions and answers that only partially fit – always also *passing* and *talking past one another*. Here the important question arises as to how to determine *deficiency* and *excess* precisely, how they can be delimited. Addressing *both* in a correlative way: Reality itself is ambivalent.'[170]

For Waldenfels, too, the central question is: How does something arise? One answer may be organic growth and organic evolution. Yet what conditions Nature? The natural sciences pursue this question, finding out the durability of the strength of their evidence, discovering the resistance of their subject matter. Is this question necessary, needed for conducting our own lives? Jullien devotes himself to it, in his Éléments d'une philosophie du vivre ('Elements of a philosophy of living'). It is addressed tout court to the modern way of thinking about creation in the West. For there is a moment in which Nature is no longer considered to be the source of truth but, rather – in the transition to the European modern era, with thinkers like Francis Bacon and René Descartes – as truth that can be proven. At that moment, a kind of productive suspicion pushes into the ancient way of understanding the world as feeling at home in the cosmos. That will lead to the proof that humanity can indeed fly even though it is naturally impossible, but it will also expose any *resource*, any *fund* to human experimentation, until the fact is recognised that 'ecosystems', that the 'atmosphere' itself has been attacked.[171]

This 'productive suspicion' informs the dynamisation of Western modernity altogether. In the eighteenth century, above and beyond the natural sciences, its theoretical grounding can be found in the rise of capitalism (in the 'parasitic' relationship of 'capital' to 'labour') and in the radicalisation of Classical inventiveness in poetics and rhetoric into aesthetic *art*. Thus, it no longer distinguishes itself *inside* art forms by way of *coming upon, finding* something but instead by *coming up with, inventing* something, through *breaks* with what exists, ruptures that prescribe a *new rule*, not just a further variation and/or an inherent possibility for development. Modern science, capitalism, *art* are all forms of *indirect* productivity, which together call the 'fund' of Nature into question, whether as a result of experiments, overexploitation, or the displacement of the 'beauty of Nature' with the 'beauty of Art'. They are part of the same adventure, one in favour of overcoming natural limits ('humans *can* fly'), to the benefit of greater independence from Nature in our standard of living ('strawberries in winter'), in support of cultivating our own imagination as the linchpin for the inventiveness of indirect ways for creating indirectly. This break-up constitutes a break-in of metaphysical exteriority into our own lifeworld: The thought of an *outside* of Nature – as God or his likeness, humankind – is made useful *in* Nature, in that *it* is stylised into something outside. At the moment in which the metaphysical body of thought itself loses strength, during the Enlightenment, in the turn towards transcendental philosophy, that thought breaks new ground in worldly form, the idea of an *outside* is transposed anew, between *humanity and Nature*. And in its expansive dynamisation from the colonisation of imperialism to the current globalisation, this process has reached every continent and challenged every culture.[172] The 'fund of Nature' today is a weave that can break, not an entity acting coherently.[173] It is here that thinking of natural immanence runs into its limits.

Thus, traditional Chinese thinking can only partially point out alternatives. Yet the radicalisation of inventiveness – whether as an experimental challenge, overexploitation, or advanced *art* – has had intensification as a consequence, which has shown its questionable sides in the threat to our bases for life, in the exploitation of resources, or in the postmodern exhaustion/idling of a permanent escalation in modern 'isms'. We need, therefore, to find another way, above and beyond the solely traditional frame of reference *and* radicalisation.

Art and anthropology

Waldenfels recommends going *between opposites*. The *Little girl with dead bird* stands in-between opposites; as a picture itself, it is one of transition. As an image, it arose – as part of a larger painting – before its radicalisation into *Art*. At the same time, it cannot be integrated into any tradition, for as a fragment it marks the singular, initial example – as an allegory of life and death – of a marginal genre that turned much more erotic later on. To what extent can this picture help today in possibly thinking differently about the mere distinction between art forms in general and *Art*? And: Do we even have to make this distinction at all? Is it not more meaningful – in the sense of Hans Belting – to speak of an anthropology of images instead? And would that not come to accommodate the anthropological approach of my considerations?

Three conceptualisations need to be distinguished here: The first is the *epistemological* one vis-à-vis the modern radicalisation of inventiveness in its various disciplines (the natural sciences, economics, philosophy of art); it had its start with Husserl's essay on the *Crisis of European sciences* (German publ. 1936, English trans. in 1954) and was pursued in particular by Rudolf Boehm, with his writings *Kritik der Grundlagen des Zeitalters* ('Critique of the foundations of the epoch' [1973]) and the slender yet exquisite volume Ökonomie und Metaphysik ('Economics and metaphysics' [2004]). In this epistemological context, Merleau-Ponty in particular expressed his views on art, in describing it as an effective alternative to science in 1961: According to Merleau-Ponty, science causes *living* in the world to be forgotten, the lifeworld as a habitat that is not to be confused with labour and what is constructed. Merleau-Ponty thus occupies a key position. For how can he treat *Art* as an advanced, cutting-edge form of the problems of the 'modern project', of the separation of humankind from Nature and of the radicalisation of dealing with it, up to and including the negation of Nature?

It is obvious that art today is in no way thought of as being in opposition to science any longer, and there are good reasons for that: In the first place, *Art* and modern science are children of the same thought process, of finding order that is contingent upon axioms, whether at the macro- or micro-level (whereas the physicist sought to determine the contingent laws of Nature rationally, the natural genius gave *Art* its contingent 'rules'); secondly, at least since the 1960s, a preponderance of communicativity has prevailed in the area of art vis-à-vis the aspect of the silence and the materiality of *Art* (while Adorno was still praising the resistant materiality of the artwork, Andy Warhol had already celebrated the interview as an art form); third, by way of technological developments and dominance, artistic forms of expression have in the meantime been fit into mathematic calculations in an intensified way – each and every digitised picture is formulated, re-presented – in other words, a vectorial playground; in the fourth place, economising in the market pushes the areas of research and art towards one another: The university as well as the art business have to 'turn a profit', and project applications for grant monies in the sciences and the arts at this point resemble each other, not least of all because the state – the sponsor they frequently share, at least in Europe – has to budget more austerely itself; fifth, the prosperous society – in which consumption and Pop Art once flourished – is in crisis. Now, after the 'culture of fun', the 'gravitas of life' has apparently returned – in other words, scientific seriousness has come back to the artistic life.

So much for the situation today and for the changed point of view on Merleau-Ponty's rejoinder for *Art* and science. Nevertheless, there are also reasons for understanding *Art* not just as a dilemma – even if today it portrays itself to some in such a way as being at all still delineated, still determined within these difficulties. In this regard, Jacques Rancière has been working on the *second* important conceptualisation, the aesthetic one. He understands what appears to be radicalisation, on the one hand, as the liberation of the arts from a set of rules for inventiveness which corresponded to social hierarchies. With the French Revolution, the introduction of democratic sensibilities, and the necessity of self-determination, people had to provide new rules for themselves, rules that no longer satisfied one absolute benchmark but instead also had to make the further rediscovery of them possible, from generation to generation, past any complete acceptance by way of *one* point of view, *one* ruler. That is, with the fall of metaphysical, monarchistic, aristocratic hierarchies, their old set of rules for inventiveness could not remain unaffected. Rather, an artistic inventiveness was required here, too, one that was likewise not determined by the particular power and direct exercise of technological competence, by *ability*, but instead by rediscoveries, *inventions*, whose creation would be thanks to an *indirect* process – the way Immanuel Kant had described it in his *Critique of Judgement*, in the section on the faculty of 'genius'. It was not until around the nineteenth century, after Friedrich Schiller changed the concept to one that was 'human', that it would develop its political reference not only to freedom but also to equality and to 'fraternity', solidarity. Then, for the first time, in the framework of the French labour movement, *Art* was spoken of as being the *avant-garde*, as the *trailblazer* for new ideas, for liberating ways of seeing, for free imagination. In that way, *Art* turns into the linchpin for *free* activity, as the source and residue of *free* ideas. Only their cultivation can lead to the democratic dynamics of the *free formation* of ideas, which calls upon *everyone*, where all are seen as *equal* in the possibility for that creation. As a result, a kind of participation, a being in connection and solidarity with certain ideas comes into play, as the social dynamics that is also inherently stimulated by the *free, liberal arts*. They constitute a form that is increasingly critical, even though in their case it involves ways of seeing that cannot be derived – like, for instance, variations. Instead, they represent *breaks* with what is well known, *new* ways of seeing, *visual kinds of knowledge*. For instance, the central perspective had been passed down for centuries as a solution for achieving the effect of depth on a flat surface. In the end, however, the Impressionists achieved that effect of depth without lines but instead via colour contrasts, and the Cubists with novel linear illusions of depth without any central perspective. If nothing else, the modern emphasis on *style* was connected with the new 'rules', new 'ways' of seeing that style made possible. Precisely in the first half of the twentieth century was when artists passionately signed up for this artistic understanding, with manifestos and stylistic concepts – from Impressionism to Symbolism to Fauvism and Cubism, Dadaism, Expressionism, Surrealism, up to and including Situationism. The decrease in stylistic developments in this regard did not denote any weakening in the *democratic* substance of art, only a change in the possible 'rules' and 'ways of seeing' that art offers. The critical impulse is still preserved; only in that regard can *Art* distinguish itself at all from other created products, from spaces, media, objects, and events that are no less cultivated. In the process, this impulse has to extend all the way to the preconditions for our own action and put them *at our disposal as well*. Art thus is a level of quality *in artistic forms*, which appears exemplary in works whenever they no longer satisfy the expectations for their respective forms (being able to recognise a handbag still as a handbag, however imaginatively and deconstructed it is created). Their quality is manifest, rather, when they *break* those expectations, by *forcing* re-orientation, by way of ambivalence, ambiguity, which in the most extreme case requires a *different* understanding of the entire *field*, like the introduction of the ready-made by Marcel Duchamp.

Reality is ambivalent – Waldenfels remarked – and art creates ambivalence, to the benefit of the freedom of the imagination, the freedom of movement in acting – as Blumenberg believed – for human beings *have to act, without being able to look past their situation*. Even if art makes only dealing indirectly with the situation possible, in pictures, this interaction is still part of the freedom of movement on the whole and nurtures the capacity for that movement, and thus in turn its orientation as well, the practical influence, the scientific demonstration.

At the same time the notion that *reality is ambivalent* – given our knowledge of the earth's astonishing exceptional status and its potential for life – recalls the necessity of an *atmosphere*, of a *resource*, a *fund*, a *lifeworld* for the regeneration of this possibility, *with which* even humanity is able only to regenerate. Caring for this *fund* is what concerns the critique of modern radicalisation. Like François Jullien, we may draw inspiration from Ancient Chinese tradition, yet the way can only lead beyond it. In this case, are we helped at all by the *third* conceptualisation that still needs to be discussed, namely, the anthropological one and, more specifically – with a view to *Art* and artistic forms – the *anthropology of images*?

As Tugendhat writes, philosophical and ethnological anthropology are distinguished by the general question into the distinction between humans and animals, and his answer for this distinction is related to language: Whereas animals communicate with signals in a way that is specific to the situation, human language allows not only for connoting objects in that situation but also for comprehending the situation itself as an object.[174] As a result, a difference to that situation arises, which can lead all the way to independence from it, to speaking of the *in itself*. Pictures possess their primary significance in representation – something was, has been perceived, disappeared; yet in being perceived an image could be retained, painted – attesting further to what had passed away, showing it representationally, putting forth what is absent as still being present, presenting the situation *as such*. This transfer function from pre- to ab-sent succeeds only in still *being able to recognise* what was past, what is only visually present. The primary requirement for the picture is therefore the quality it possesses to re-present, to give again. It gives something back, places something at our disposal that has itself eluded being held onto, something that passes away. We can be thankful for a picture, a memory, a testament. That enables our own continuity and identity – what would we be without our memories? For a long time the capacity for representation, for concentrated commensurability vis-à-vis a situation, a circumstance, also determined our understanding of artistic forms. It defined their quality of 'vivid recognition', as Aristotle laid out in his *Poetics*, for instance – that they ensure insight, create understanding, for human questions in general – like in tragedy, for example. It was in the *linguistic* quality of the picture, in the *language* of the image – the imagery in which what was absent is posited as present, on the stage of the *in itself* – that the significance of artistic forms was exemplified.

The relationship between philosophical and ethnological anthropology, then, is revealed in how that which characterises humanity as such has found its shape in various cultures. In this context, Hans Belting considers the 'images of the dead' to be the central motivation for 'human picture-making', moreover observing that only an anthropological perspective might address these topics.'[175] That is already clear insofar as talking about *Art* – and thus about art history, too – only came about in the eighteenth century. That is true, too, for the need to interrogate past artistic forms regarding their possible inclusion under the new criteria for *Art* – the way undertaken in 1764 by Johann Joachim Winckelmann, as the founder of art history, with his programmatic interpretation of Ancient Greek artworks. Whereas *Art* and its history, in accordance with its own paradigm for *free imagination*, always gave precedence to the individual – whether as 'producer', 'receiver', or 'work' – the emphasis in ethnological collections is always on the culture, and thus on the cultural and collective memory. Whereas collections of Western *Art* emphasise the personal and individual (the signature of the artist), presentation in ethnological museums ofter has a 'supra-personal' effect, homogenising into 'groups' or even anonymously. The problems of an ethnology informed by the West have been addressed multiple times. For the anthropology of images the same questions arise.

With a view to the *Little girl with dead bird*, I have tried to demonstrate the anthropological dimension by way of intercultural comparison with traditionally Chinese thinking, while exercising all the caution demanded when we seek to *alteritise* our own standpoint within the context of a Western tradition. We want to understand the parameters of another way of thinking in order to describe the picture within those possibilities. In these anthropological implications, it can be thoroughly seen not as an 'image of the dead', but as an image of life and death; after all, both elements are fundamental questions for all humans, no matter how individuals, families, groups, and societies deal with either phenomenon.

After this intercultural comparison, we additionally questioned how alternatives in thought open up via going back to traditions and beyond their radicalisation. And for observing images that means: How do these open up via going back to traditional artistic forms and beyond their radicalisation into *Art*? In order to escape polarisations and mere opposition, Waldenfels preferred *going in-between* as an opening, *between* the supposed opposites, just as he distinguishes *passio* between passivity and activity, or the *element* between matter and form. Is there also a *moment in-between* artistic forms on the one hand and *Art* on the other, a *moment in-between* poetics and rhetoric versus aesthetics and the philosophy of art? And can gazing upon the painting *Little girl with dead bird* – a picture from a transitional era, from the beginning of the intellectual emancipation of artistic forms since the Renaissance all the way to the formulation of the claim for *Art* during the Enlightenment – contribute to clarifying this question?

How does the picture present itself as an artistic form? It is an oil painting, on an oak panel, measuring 36.7×29.8 cm, unsigned, dating around 1520, in the South Netherlandish style. It was likely part of a group portrait, out of which it alone has remained intact. Neither the circumstances of its creation nor its later reworking are known. It is the first examplar connecting the figure of a girl with that of a dead bird. A passage in Catullus can be offered as an iconographic reference; it was that reference that provided the erotic variation of this motif handed down later on. This allegorical version without any erotic connotation cannot be found any further, however; to all appearances, it is a unique find. In that sense, the picture attests to an innovation in terms of motif, via technical and stylistic means known since the Renaissance. During the Renaissance, a change in artistic and art-theoretical poetics took place, whereby the properties of a picture were no longer noted as *inventio*, as invention, but instead as *trovare*, accentuating what is *new* as well. That was only possible because the status of the picture had changed.

As handed down in the framework of Aristotelian ontology, an image did not acquire the status of anything substantive; it always remained characterised by the 'as-if' – only what was naturally substantial possessed the strength for renewal, regeneration, whereby here, too, the question about what is new in terms of evolution surfaced at most on the margins (in the question as to couplings amongst animals which were possible, yet did not have the capacity to procreate). What is 'new' was not any deciding criterion in Aristotelian poetics. If we were to interpret the *Little girl with dead bird* against this backdrop, then we would have to ascertain the framework for possible denotations. The object of the image could concern either the dimensions of what is existing and what has been; or the statements and opinions about what is existing; or those of its desirable, ideal form.[176] The motif of the fragment at hand is a girl with a dead bird. Are these two idealised? No. Do they reflect opinions and notions? No, the motif cannot be traced back to that but, rather, presents in fact something not so very well known for that time. Does it show what is existing and what has been? Yes, it does so explicitly, to be sure, symbolised by two figures. It is an allegory of what is existing and what has been, in the form of a young girl – a symbol for the beginning of life (based on her physical constitution, which allows for an expectation of maturing) – and in the form of a dead bird – as the breakdown of that vitality. The *language* of the image is clearly recognisable, both in the figurative as well as in the metaphorical sense. The execution precisely corresponds to that exactness, commensurability, that Aristotle had expected from an artistic work: The artist has committed neither 'accidental' mistakes in the portrayal (*if* we are working within the dimension of what is existing and what has been, *then* we had better be exact in that regard and evoke a *realistic* impression). Nor did he make any 'substantial' error, such that he would not measure up to his own intention, whether in his technical expertise or intellectual fullness. The artist has also avoided additional, possible mistakes in accordance with the understanding of poetics: He does not show anything impossible (the question as to idealisation is ruled out in this case), works 'truthfully', refrains in that regard also from giving opinions about his motif of life and death, by portraying the child without any chain with a crucifix, in not showing any religious symbols in the space, and so on. In this way, to be sure, the child's *situation* does not become clear, yet her gaze opens up the visual space onto a different horizon, one that is outside the picture, further behind the observer, as the gaze into the distance obliquely goes over the shoulder of the one observing. *Where* is the girl gazing? Is she gazing upon something specific? These *situational* questions take the picture as their point of departure in equal measure. In this sense, it could be interpreted even in advance of the premises of Classical thought, in that it coherently cultivates contradiction (death and life), identity (of the child), and the 'excluded Third Party' (the viewpoint). This coherence suffices for both the impression of an image *from reality* as well as for claims to a realistic *portrayal* – since this was obviously strived for – in other words, the *concentration* of reality into *one* picture, *one* composition. This entity is accorded special significance. For as an artificial construction and a successful ensemble, it symbolises above and beyond that the entirety of reality. The concentration on *one* image can be understood as concentrating on *one* section – or on the totality. On the one hand, the *Little girl with dead bird* shows a snippet from one possible reality in which a child holds a dead bird in her hands and looks up, questioning. At the same time, the abstract background contradicts the pure realism and in that way emphasises an allegorical reading of the picture. In that interpretation, what has been – in the shape of the bird – is at the lower edge of the picture, while the picture itself is filled with that which is existing from the child, from whom a gaze into the distance also expands the temporal components of what has been and what is existing, all the way into the future. *Shall* I grow up? Am I as fragile as a little bird? What awaits me? Surely the same fate, just like the bird? Am I a life from the same life? Mortal the way it is?

According to traditional poetics, then, these kinds of questions would have been involved. Artistic forms pertained to the production of the image – according to Aristotle, the poet is as much a *creator* as the painter or comparable artists – and these images are the focus of expectations that have been handed down. With a view to an artist's expertise, the unique special features of each and every medium is taken as the point of departure – poetry, painting, and so on. At the same time, this assumption meant that a statue was expected in the framework of sculpting, a tragedy in the framework of poetry – no different to expecting a sprint in a race, for instance, and a gunfight in a duel. There was no playing around with these expectations. They could only be satisfied, however, when they led to an exciting struggle in sport, and to a touching as well as understandable result in the arts. And nothing that was adequately known and demonstrated would be experienced as being 'exciting' or 'touching'. Inventiveness on the part of actors, therefore, pertained to *seeing* things *differently* to what is expected. In sport, this ingenuity became clear based on the rules of the game: On a playing field actors are able to act in accordance with the same rules known for generations. Excitement can only arise as a result of the actors' situational inventiveness and can only increase if especially daring actions emerge, if configurations become concentrated, if the unpredictable of any given game causes what is familiar in its rules to be forgotten, and *via* these rules something excessive comes into play that enthrals the public. There is something comparable in theatrical performances. At a premiere, the audience is familiar with the genre – tragedy, comedy – and with the rules, the play, the actors. It is up to the actors to create, *via* these rules, something excessive for this unique situation, which will enchant the audience, enthral it. And in painting? It would also be judged according to the criteria Aristotle laid out, and as I have demonstrated by way of example with the picture of the *Little girl with dead bird*. We could have interpreted it – had it been already well known– completely in accordance with these rules, so as to be able to enjoy the portrayal itself *via* them. Could it have been related as an allegory to a literary source in Ancient Greece, as it was in Ancient Rome with Catullus? Or how would our discussion have looked for an alternative *genre*? In poetry, as a generic term, there were similarly introductions of alternative types, like comedy, for instance. The daring *genre*, therefore, would have to make the understanding of the image in the Classical sense no more difficult. It would only have been capable of being integrated, though, not as something *new* but, rather, as something invented, something *found* within the properties of what is possible, yet always limited.

On the one hand, the Renaissance goes back to this tradition; on the other, above and beyond it. What distinction to *inventio* does the key term *trovare* mark? Both have to do with finding. After breaking with the representative arts of Antiquity via the artistic forms of the Middle Ages, going back to them seamlessly is no longer possible; the space for their properties, their 'fundus', is temporally removed and only present in the ruins of the architecture and the broken pieces of the artefacts that stand in for them. The 'world of Antiquity' needs to be 'discovered' again, and this perspective is distinguished from the self-understood nature of that world. *Discovering* becomes the key concept of another kind of finding, a finding not in what is given but, rather, in what is forsaken, forlorn, forgotten, what is no longer within 'arm's reach' of what is possible. It is no longer within the 'fundus' of 'our own culture' but instead exists in relation to cultures that have gone under, that of Ancient Rome and its source of inspiration, Ancient Greece. Here, then, rediscovery, renewal must be thought of against the backdrop of a break. And this break is of an historical sort, distinct from evolutionary, organic change, for instance. When the painters, sculptors, and architects of the Renaissance reach back to the central perspective of Ancient Greece, it is also in order to effect an emancipation of its arts with it, in which *discovering* – in the case of Leon Battista Alberti, for instance – is associated with *sketching*, just as careful *judgement* is associated with the composed *design* and the *selection* of the line of thought with the *portrayal* of an action, spatially and visually.[177] The break, which is first determined by discovering, determines from then on also how finding is accentuated as re-finding, like re-opening – namely, in the re-newing of our own standpoint. Only given the increasing critique of Aristotelian ontology, in fact – on the part of Descartes or the later Kant – will it arrive at a revision of this differentiating *to the benefit of what is new*. Still, the Renaissance is the beginning of this development.

The *Little girl with dead bird* is not portrayed in the manner of the Late Gothic, in the way the era of the elder Cranach, for instance, still painted figures. Instead, in terms of perspective, she is portrayed exactly, 'truthfully', in accordance with Nature, in her embodiment as well as her vitality. The girl makes a realistic impression on us; the bird could be 'real'. Painted in the South Netherlandish style, it is an image in the spirit of the Renaissance, as the art historian Bob Claessens emphatically pointed out.

Art is a quality *in* artistic forms, a radicalisation of its inventiveness for having a much more *indirect*, dissociative, critical effect, in order to change our understanding of the forms themselves, if possible, our understanding of their media, their field, their history. Its critique is always cognitive: challenging knowledge that is well known, perception and imagination that are familiar. Is the *Little girl with dead bird* this kind of 'provocation'? Does it change our view of *Art*? No. It is a singular invention in Art, having founded a genre in painting, one that to this day is hardly well known, let alone researched. It is a 'prototype', a refinding. It does not put the limits of the recognisable forms and their classifiability into question, nor those of its medium much less those of its 'field'; it follows tradition in this. Yet it creates a new connection to them, one that only still exists as such and hardly entails any discernible weave – only an initial, loose thread, a fragile possibility, *trovare*. It leads into the *in-between* of radical *Art* and the 'pleasant', stimulating, understandable artistic form. This *in-between* opens up out of the shape of the child, the way the arms hold the bird downward from the child's body, in her strangely greyish hands, and the face directs the gaze upward from the child's bonnet and the shadows into the distance, tightly, her mouth closed, a delicate line of firmess, of trust, continuing to the question that demands courage, the entire gravitas of a child asking herself the question, not running away or crying, still just barely keeping her sense of balance, with the animal in her hands, her eyes looking up, with her faint eyebrows, dashes, in the plasticity of her face, of her slightly red cheeks, of her temples in the shadows, of her tightly covered hair, without any strands – the earnestness speaks from every detail. She seems to possess a steadfast character, which speaks from her composition: from the body at rest, the arms framing her body and resting quietly on her lap, or possibly a table, almost on the lower edge of the picture. Quiet is the mood of balance, of equilibrium, and not just that of an even temper. In the quiet inheres a tension, which her questioning gaze conveys. It is not a form that rests *in and of itself*. The uncertainty, the question, demands a kind of seeing that does not simply resist it, one that observes, that fixes its place. The child is abandoned, left to her circumstances. Yet she looks between confidence and concern – as though everything depends on the answer to come, which steers the gaze towards it. An adult who sets her mind at rest? An older child, laughing at her: *What do you care about a dead bird?!* A younger child who does not understand? A bird hopping away from her? A tree with its branches moving in the wind?

The question regarding Merleau-Ponty was whether a different understanding of *Art* could also be obtained from this *in-between*, above and beyond its effect as a solely aesthetic paradigm in 'productive suspicion'. For it was Merleau-Ponty who saw in art precisely the possibility of a distance to this prevailing modern paradigm. In so doing, he did not take as his point of departure an oppositional principle like that of subject and object, humanity and world. Instead, he inquired after that which made the positing – that is, even that of opposites – possible at all in the first place. Making this possible cannot be sought in any external entity (by which an undecidable regress of ultimate justification would arise); rather, it must be presumed in the differentiation of that which makes a relation manifest. As was already mentioned at the outset, Merleau-Ponty took inspiration here from Gestalt theory, in which the visual phenomenon of a contrast is analysed, by which a figure and its concurrently appearing ground separate. This contrast is not preceded by any entity, any source or truth. In the separation of the dominant and the concurrently apparent, both arise only *in* their relationship to one another and *as* such a relationship. As a contrast, then, Merleau-Ponty – like Waldenfels after him – attempts to grasp the relationship between humanity and world, *with* which relatable points, opposites, and so forth first arise.

Human beings are physically part of the world, just as 'the world is made of the very stuff of the body', Merleau-Ponty writes in *Eye and mind*.[178] In the movement of humanity, there is continual crisscrossing and intertwining between its own and alien materiality. This contrasting differentiates our own particular body, which we possess, with its permanently interwoven nature in the generally material element. This interwovenness can be sensed, for instance, in how I perceive my voice in space – as an echo of my physicality and that of the space. According to Merleau-Ponty, this sensing is not a purely physical one that can be isolated but, rather a corporeal one, a feeling. Artists work from this intuition when they test and present possibilities for differentiating this interwovenness in a vivid manner. The problems of painting, as he writes, 'illustrate the enigma of the body, which enigma in turn legitimates them.'[179] And that means: 'In paintings themselves we could seek a figured philosophy of vision.'[180]

According to this approach, the crisis in the natural sciences would come from taking relational models *as the point of departure*, testing them by means of something alien to them, rather than starting from their contrasts with the world, which would first make the formation of autonomous models possible. The question is whether this objection can still be raised today, if one follows through on writings regarding the epistemology of the natural sciences, like those of Hans-Jörg Rheinberger. In his *Epistemology of the concrete*, he describes at length how we came to construct an experimental system from analysis of the scientific set of tools, a system that allows the effects of what is unforeseeable to be detected and, as a result, shifts in what has already been apprehended to be demonstrated and interpreted.[181] It is not the model that comes at the beginning but, rather, the instruments themselves – what does a microscope, for instance, allow us to discover? Even after Merleau-Ponty's critical analysis, however, the question still remains as to whether this might only shift the problem from logical hypotheses to techniques we can construct. Rheinberger, at least, always considers these techniques to be *phenomenotechniques* (borrowing the term from Gaston Bachelard), based on their being adapted to human operation and physicality.[182] Yet a notion of how this physicality is 'interwoven' with the investigatory world has not been elaborated.

In this sense, the natural sciences do not comparably operate from the 'lived corporeality' as the arts do, for corporeality in the arts is oriented *in* the interwoven nature of our own materiality and that of the world, whereas in the natural sciences this materiality encounters what is alien only within instrumental *settings*. In this way, we might argue for another difference between art and science.

The paradigm of a 'productive suspicion' must be maintained for art, if we want to remain true to the critical claim it shares with other disciplines of modernity. Yet the possibility of transposing art via mere radicalisation of this suspicion and intensification of the interplay between destruction and construction into regenerative, artistic action and thought can only be based in contrasting, revealing the *axioms* of this process of differentiation in acting. According to Merleau-Ponty, this 'zero point' of the process would be corporeal interwovenness. Rancière, for instance, would in turn see that condition in particular in 'equality', that is, in the equality of all participants in the process, in the sense that every human being masters language and everything that is composed linguistically – like the languages of images, for example – can potentially be understood. Another ideal of the Enlightenment, liberty, is similarly entangled with art and, like equality in its additionally political significance, it requires the acknowledgement of free imagination for the acknowledgement of any art that it cultivates. And, like Merleau-Ponty – despite their distinctive ways of thinking – Rancière understands the regenerative or, as he calls it, the emancipatory moment of what the artist does in *returning to the point of departure*. The meandering movement of conversion, change, deformation, destruction, repetition, assemblage, collage, construction, montage – all the possible, extending, differentiating ways of acting in artistic practices, which stir up, disturb, crisscross, transform what exists via that suspicion – they are no longer ends in themselves at that moment, since they make the corporeal experience, the equality, liberty, and other 'zero points' of their process always appear anew as well, as elements of the game, without which that game itself cannot be productive.

In this way, Merleau-Ponty's essay *Eye and mind* can be read as the portrayal of an example as to how art can remain true to its critical, innovating claim, to its self-referentiality, *inasmuch* as it makes visible by which complements this effect can only be achieved. Thus, art is neither autonomous nor dependent on something external to it; it arises only in contrast to certain elements. As a figure that can be experienced, it stands out from its otherwise invisible ground.

Does the *Little girl with dead bird* reveal something of this ground? Can it only be described as innovation in a limited way itself? If it is not also an artistic revolution, not even a revolt, then this certainly is based on its subject, life and death, which forbids taking any mere action, unmasking its own influence as hybris. What does being artistically revolutionary matter in the case of a topic that only deflects any dexterity, that is unchangeable, an anthropological stigma of mortality? The grand gesture does not count here, and even if the picture's painter could not yet know anything of all the revolutionary discourses of modernity, he still knew very precisely what stance was needed to portray such a topic, in a thoroughly innovative way, in varying a well-known motif of joy – the baby Jesus with the bird, for example – as a visual finding apart from the well-known genre, and yet without emphasised pathos, without action, concentrated down to the details exactly, without becoming sterile and fastidious but, rather, balancing between connotation and execution, gesture and distance. The *ground* of that which is made manifest as the stance in the shape of the girl is a certain relationship to mortality, a gravitas that touches upon individual integrity. *How do you deal with the question what does death mean – and life?*

The complements of art are multi-faceted: anthropological in the case of our own interwovenness with the world, mortality, or generically determined equality; democratic as in the case of liberty. There is a broader way for demonstrating how these complements are differentiated in their approaches from artistic forms and art. The element of mortality has accompanied the arts since the first prehistoric forms of burial; the moment of liberty is a motif of the Enlightenment, regarding Greek Antiquity. With anthropology, therefore, thinking about these complements would have to set in, as Hans Belting has shown in his anthropology of images and in the relationship between image and death. Yet the anthropology of images ultimately would have to be apprehended in a way that complements *Art*, in the sense of how elements are shown with it, which even in critical art are still complementary in significance and which, in accordance with 'productive suspicion', lead to historically and situationally corresponding figures and forms. In this manner, a picture from the sixteenth century and one from today would be thoroughly comparable. *Little girl with dead bird* is a sixteenth-century form, turned into a complement, a ground of anthropological significance – and in doing so is once again close to us. Thus, it is about integrating art into the triad of artistic forms, *Art*, and the anthropology of images, with a view to the conditions for the picture's protean nature.

Thoughts on life and death (III)

'Division into sky and earth–/it's not the proper way/to contemplate this wholeness./It simply lets me go on living' – Wisława Szymborska.[183] Opposition does not suffice in contemplating 'wholeness' – does it let us to 'go on living'? Geometry, mathematics, logic, technology? The wholeness does not lead outside the points opposed but, rather, into them, into the interwovenness with the world. It is only in this way that Merleau-Ponty's very telling remark can be understood: '[O]ne cannot judge the powers of life by those of death, nor define without arbitrariness life as the sum of the forces that resist death (...).'[184] For making the opposite absolute leads into an assumed bottomlessness, an abyss that does not exist; as Bernhard Waldenfels remarks, it would result, rather, from the 'dissolution of scientific constructions and their transition to autonomy', namely, in the *construction* of an 'objectivism'.[185] This construction becomes necessary when mythological explanations no longer endure – Anaximander had already begun that constructing, when he drafted a model of the cosmos that, according to Ludger Schwarte, was not based 'any longer on an origin myth [...] but, rather on mutual foundational connections', between heaven, earth, and sun.[186] The construction, however, is itself only a part of overcoming the problem. Its becoming autonomous would be – and is – itself a problem. For the construction operates – and this remains the critical point – with conditions that it itself cannot provide. In order to achieve any 'surviving' not opposed to but, rather, with these conditions, it requires the contrast between 'oxygen' and 'air', though the one is owing to a construction in regard of the other.[187] In this sense, the matter is more complex than when François Jullien states that a 'philosophy of breathing' is supposedly outside the scope of *every* Western philosophy, even outside phenomenology.[188] In *Eye and mind*, this interwovenness, the 'flesh', the 'texture' of what exists is described by Merleau-Ponty as the 'inspiration and expiration of Being'.[189] This breathing takes place precisely on the other side of a split into subject and object, because 'action and passion' cannot be distinguished from one another any longer, and we find ourselves instead in an 'element' that also constitutes us, is not outside but extends far beyond us, and creates its existence out of atmospheric conditions other than those we can generate. Under certain circumstances, this thinking would come completely close to a 'philosophy of breathing'. Yet at the same time it itself is contrasted with efforts taken to influence what is happening, characterised by the 'productive suspicion' that has made it possible to construct aeroplanes even though human beings cannot fly, and to take along oxygen even where human beings cannot breathe. Any possible 'philosophy of breathing' must be in line with this critical turning point, if it intends to have recourse not only to traditional Asian thought but also to modernity and the present in the East as well as the West.

* * *

In introducing these considerations, I wrote that I wished to treat 'three decisive questions' with a view to the motif of life and death: *one fundamentally concerns the relationship to 'belief', the other the relationship between life and death – and the third whether and how both questions are related to each other.*

The first question on belief appears to me to be so comprehensively discussed as to have found its essential point in the phenomenon of the gaze between the individual dying and the one attending that death. For Ricœur as well as for Levinas, religiosity is sparked by this gaze, particularly by the condition of being-seen ('*Gesehenwerden*'), a traditionally religious topos. With both philosophers, the interpretation of this gaze leads past phenomenology to hermeneutics or, as the case may be, into radically responsive thinking. I do not share this step past the phenomenology of the gaze that is still present – derived though this move is from religious sources alone. The phenomenology of this gaze, however, does not rule out any such step or exclude any such understanding. In order to exclude it, we – like Tugendhat – have to make reference to another method of argumentation. Yet it does not appear to be compelling to me, as I presented in comparison with Ricœur. In this regard, phenomenologically speaking, I remain caught between renouncing and affirming religious faith and, ethically speaking, permit myself precisely this kind of candour.

I want to observe the relationship between life and death one more time in terms of the question of death. Paul Ricœur writes: 'There is first of all the encounter of the death of a loved other' – and even if in doing so it only involves a bird, an animal, a playmate – 'of unknown others. Someone has disappeared. (...) This question connects death with the dead person, the dead ones. It is a question for the living.'[190] It may appear banal that death only comes into being with life, yet in that way death is always only a matter of those living, and its transfer to any hereafter only succeeds when life is transferred there. This evident 'hereafter', however, is only the lifeless matter in space, distant from all complementarity between life and death. This distance, this infinity is unimaginable – it appears to be spatial, yet it eludes every distinction into inside and outside. This cosmic infinity concerns me only in confounding it with permanence – my body is permanently present, my consciousness is dreaming even while asleep. In this way Szymborska is able to make the paradoxical formulation: 'I'd rather think / that I'd temporarily died / than that I kept on living / And can't remember a thing.'[191] We can lose consciousness, awaken from a coma, find explanations, for our own absence – but a tabula rasa of our own permanence is impossible. And yet therein lies the greatest contrast between life and death, namely, that with birth death is written into our cellular circuitry, into the development of our nerves, the resilience of our blood vessels, the years that the ensemble just holds together. A provisory body, brimming with lust and desire. A time span. The poetess thus writes of being 'Trapped from birth in departing bodies',[192] and dedicates to them a poem of their own, "Nothing's a gift": 'Nothing's a gift, it's all on loan. / I'm drowning in debts up to my ears. / I'll have to pay for myself / with myself, / give up my life for my life. // Here's how it's arranged: / The heart can be repossessed, / the liver, too, / and each single finger and toe. // Too late to tear up the terms, / my debts will be repaid, / and I'll be fleeced, / or, more precisely, flayed. // I move about the planet / in a crush of other debtors. / Some are saddled with the burden / of paying off their wings. / Other must, willy-nilly, / account for every leaf. // Every tissue in us lies / on the debit side. / Not a tentacle or tendril / is for keeps. // The inventory, infinitely detailed, / implies we'll be left / not just empty-handed, / but handless, too. // I can't remember / where, when, and why / I let someone open / this account in my name. // We call the protest against this / the soul. / And it's the only item / not included on the list.'[193]

If the soul is nothing more than a bundle of nerves, that is, the energy that is recognisable, that becomes perceptible as the totality of its components, as drive, instinct, resistance, fear, and need, then even this totality cannot be saved from being caught between life and death but, rather, is mobilised precisely as its own antipole towards the transitory nature of its component matter. The threat to the *totality*, to the *whole*, at the same time mobilises it into *wanting* life. Thus, for instance, Tugendhat remarks: 'Not until we see our fear of death as the flip-side of the will to continue living are we able to understand why we do not sense this fear from a distance. The will to continue living is always concerned with the next phase of life; it is not any will to live floating above us as such.'[194] Only consciousness is free-floating, the awareness 'that we will die at some time or another, or that we can die at any time (...).'¹⁹⁵ In that case, this consciousness is only a kind of creeping dread, a fear of the certainty of the coming end. It concurs with the will to continue living, on the one hand, and the fear of dying a violent death, on the other hand – of suffocating, dying like an animal, dying of thirst. In that regard, every death is violent, as Ricœur writes – a violence that is elusive, and which we canot elude, an exhaustion of our own powers, even if only while sleeping.¹⁹⁶

From this perspective, two questions arise: How do I deal with this certain finitude – and with not wanting to die *now*, but to keep on living *still*? How do I deal with the violence of death? The latter question applies above all to medical care in alleviating pain. The former concerns my understanding of self as well as my world. Tugendhat writes, for instance: 'Seen this way, death itself suggests an answer to the question it confronts, though it is not easy to apprehend that response.'¹⁹⁷ At first, it is just a matter of acknowledging our transitory nature and finitude. We practice this acknowledgement daily, vis-à-vis others whose death and oblivion does not hurt our identity, like with distant relatives, for example, from generations prior to us, whom we ourselves never knew personally, and to whom there is no longer anyone in the family to bear testimony; like with deaths in the media that remain alien to us; and so forth. Why shouldn't what we ourselves claim for others be true for us? This vitality, then, is interpersonal, having effect only in personal encounters or through stand-in testimonials – whether biographical, historical, cultural, or artistic in nature. And this interpersonal scattering, this differentiating of our own actions, speaking, appearing, is similarly finite – as René Magritte so beautifully described it, with his painting of a tombstone from the year one hundred ninety-two thousand and ...¹⁹⁸ Nobody, not even an artist, expects that in a hundred thousand years he himself or through his stand-in (by way of archaeological finds of even his works in the likely long forgotten culture) will still have any impact. Being forgotten, transitory, finite, and dead are facts we must take as our points of departure.

In view of this superior power, only relativising ourselves and our own conflict with such relativisation remains. For positing the power as absolute would be a solution, of course, but one which draws conclusions before the facts, as if it were necessary to pre-empt them. We can 'immerse' ourselves into the world, the way mystics have practised since time immemorial. And we can *allow for* the requirements of corporeal permanence – eating something – in this immersing, until apparently no distinction exists any longer between what is nourishing as nourishment and what is nourishing as a human being. Surrendering to the elements may school us in *not* resisting them, and the practice of blowing along with and being blown away by the breezy wind, which we ourselves just are, may lead to understanding ourselves precisely in doing so.[199] Yet the question still arises how we can connect this immersing with the social life of parenthood, the exchange with other cultures, or even the love for one another – as the strongest desire. For parenthood is another form of relativising ourselves, is it not? The fact that I see to the care of another life, that I can no longer understand my own life without it, that it appears even more important than my own, because it is dependent on me during those first long years? The fact that I recognise how my 'absolute' life will just be an example, the way the lives of others were for me? When I have really learned this self-relativisation in being a parent – the way we do not learn it in a comparable way by being a partner, for instance – I am still able to separate from somebody, whereas a child can only be disowned (Jean-Pierre and Luc Dardenne show this poignantly in their film *The Kid with a bike* [2011]) – then this relativisation also has consequences for our relationship with death. For whereas our own birth cannot be imagined a priori, the beginning of another life acquires an exemplary nature – before our own eyes, in growing up, learning, and developing – an exemplary role that shows us both the unique character of the child and of ourselves as well as the exemplary quality that permeates 'each and every individual life', and exemplarity that the child or the youth, the young man is not so aware of in his own momentum, in maturing, in just finding his way even. We are always in the thick of things, and everything is still ahead of us – that is how we live into the future, and also continue to live in it, simultaneously with the knowledge of finding ourselves increasingly fulfilled by it, finding ourselves in the midst of that future, in the 'middle of life', the way we hope after all. At the same time, becoming parents opens up the idea of *everything still ahead of us*, but for another individual, developing hopefully even much longer. The question of living on is deferred, as relative as that deferment may be. Yet it does exist. It defers at least the break between our own finitude in death and our own finitude in being forgotten by others, even if nothing guarantees this bridge. For what is important is not the nullification of our finitude – that is impossible – but instead how we deal with it. The deferment to the other individual opens up a kind of activity above and beyond singular action, as Hannah Arendt showed in her philosophy of natality.[200] Even so, immersing into a world – one whose ecosystems are attacked, ecosystems that Nature no longer offers as a homestead, as dependent on Nature as they may be – must appear questionable today. Yet even as untimely as it may have appeared at other times, the deferment to the Other – the sideways relativisation, as Tugendhat says – always continues to have an effect. Szymborska writes: 'The world is never ready/for the birth of a child.'[201] And Arendt composed the same thought as follows, the idea that though human beings must of course die, they 'are not born in order to die but in order to begin'.[202] This new beginning comes from the fact that there is no other totality than one that is implied, constructed; that neither the beginning nor the end of the world can be considered as clarified, but that this lack of resolution also means the quality of our own lives, for instance, is not determined by birth and death. What is new arises through coincidence, which is inherent to the contingency of the world and of humanity; it comes about through excess. Understanding the world, Nature, and humanity in an infinite, differentiating process of what is happening leads to being able not to take the atmosphere of a natural home as an assumed given; it results in seeing what is new completely as the quality of being differentiated, *yet not losing our focus on the world and Nature either*, in regard of deferment 'to the Other'. For that can involve an 'Other'. And for 'practice' in passing away it may appear more meaningful to the one individual to be practised precisely in that, in something 'other'.

The gaze between the dying individual and the one attending him is concentrated on 'the Other'. Anticipating the end itself, or thinking of it in its deferment – both these ways of dealing with it do not exclude each other, as it may appear, if we think only of the most extreme examples of it: in mysticism, on the one hand, and in the religious exaltation of what is personal, on the other. Perhaps it can also be an object, a piece of Nature, allowing one individual to share with the Other, sort of holding the hand of the dying individual.[203] I believe, though, that we are children much longer than these wisdoms suggest – whenever I think of the gesture of the girl who died in a hospital after a traffic accident, and whose last, almost unconscious, gesture was to reach for the hand of the woman sitting at her bedside, her grandmother. The grandmother is a woman maybe fifty years old, our green grocer. She told me only of the gesture, not any anecdote.

* * *

Relativising ourselves with other cultures can be seen precisely in regard of the understanding of death and life. The writings of François Jullien yet also those of Byung-Chul Han are particularly inviting for this purpose. Thus, for instance, Jullien recalls that life does not mean the same thing as ek-sistence – plants, animals, and human beings live, yet people out-line their way towards something, set goals for themselves beyond the day-to-day, *for life*. Although this perspective *towards* life does lead to the question of concern, we need to think about the fact that it is the lack of concern, carelessness, 'in which we live'.[204] While we might emphasise either the look upward ('Aufschau') in line with Heidegger or evolution in line with Taoism – as a positive turn of carelessness – in my estimation we need to attend much more to their relationship instead. In this respect, too, the phenomenological outlook is shown to be one that is between the radical retreat into life – Taoism – and ontology.

What appears to be especially convincing to me is Jullien's observation of the *moment*, as something 'intensive', as a concentration that does not measure itself by anything but lived experience, that does not have any 'starting signal' or any 'finish', the coming of which is first sensed in the having-come ('Gekommen-sein') and its going first experienced in changing. This vital moment implies nothing extraordinary, no event, no high point or break; it is a deepening, a melting of what is bundled together, a collection that expresses the infinitive: 'That means for me – *to live.*' It is this infinite thing that, according to Jullien, connects the permanence of the body as the experience of the unlimited – *in the concentrating*, in the *in-between* – with the idea of infinity, suggesting its plausibility above and beyond the logical experiment. Life lives from the infinite, from the unlimited and yet the concentrated. This concentration is not a one-sided contraction, consolidation, or tension. It is breathing the moment that withholds nothing, that does not anticipate; it is not a point we concentrate on but, rather, a 'conveyed exchange', conveyed by the air, by the element in which we move, which envelops us, *to have time*, for a day, a week, an hour. 'Living in the moment' means finding the rhythm in which the feeling sets in that *it is good the way it is*. This feeling is supported by nothing, groundless, left open to change. Found only in coming and going, though, it excludes no movement. It does not get lost, even though it is absent, and plays deep into memory. For what other 'good' memories are there than those when we had time, in childhood, with a friend, in the countryside, city, with our girlfriend, as a youth, an adult, wherever and whomever with? When I think of an aunt of mine who died – she was the cousin of my mother, so actually more distantly related – I could think of many images. Yet the image that appears closest at hand to me is when we were sitting in the living room, and she had made coffee, and I was sitting across from her, right before the 'coffee-table talk' started. She looked around the room impishly, delighted with the decorated table. I like to think of her in that moment, as fleeting as it was. Being able to enjoy that – what better opportunity do we get for being as we are when relaxed, for being able to gather ourselves together, without exertion and exercise? Gathering as relaxing, relaxing into the 'infinitive' – perhaps that is what the 'cup of coffee' is for, the 'book', the 'stroll', the 'good talk', and so on. When I think of this infinitive *'to live'*, then I do not think of ecstasy or ascetics but, rather, of the possibility of finding this gathering together in a shape, a culture, with a 'glass of wine', with concerns at a distance, in the moment that is not the best but good instead, for being able to let *things* go and enjoy *them*, so that with them something good develops.

Byung-Chul Han expresses it this way: 'Finitude (...) makes possible (...) a singular experience of time as giving.'[205] Being able to let things go means not pursuing them any further, letting them end, whether for the time being or definitively. Death or finitude is not frightening as such – the idea that *at some time* we will be dead and forgotten – but instead when it is imminent, *not now!* Finitude deferred towards the Other or into work is less frightening than having the definitive end itself before our eyes, without anyone familiar, without a trace, having surrendered only to the place where we come to an end (unless we abandon ourselves to the 'way of the world'). Ending, though, is the precondition for *letting go* – and thus also for just *receiving*. Whereas the mystic or the believer sees a possibility for renewing life in this ending – diving into the unending Becoming, or entering into eternal life with death – those who move within the philosophical tradition are asked to consider the question concerning the 'giving', life as a 'gift'. In keeping with Arendt, we could understand that it does not consist of the giving at some point being followed by its revocation but, rather, that understanding life as giving invokes 'giving further', as insight into every singularity and meaning of life, which demands a corresponding way of interacting that needs to be achieved, *thanks* to the Other – whether Nature, living being, or the world. The symbolism of this 'giving further' recognises its many forms, from cultic exaltation all the way to daily greeting of the Other with the hand.

* * *

Little girl with dead bird is a 'snapshot', the moment in one story that is completely concentrated onto that instant, a story that invokes dealing with what has happened – the girl lifts her gaze. Is it also a moment of gathering, deepening? It is not a moment in the sense of *it is good the way it is*. It is not any 'living in the moment'. The moment is undecided because it describes a conflict, between the dead animal and the girl, who is seeking how to act towards it, with her gaze. It is therefore also not the idea that *it is good the way it has been*. The girl is still too young to say farewell already and, moreover, the bird did not die a natural death. How would she react, if she had heard the following story from a distant land: 'There was once a man, Tung-mên Wu of Wei, who when his son died testified no grief. His house-steward said to him: "The love you bore your son could hardly be equalled by that of any other parent. Why, then, do you not mourn for him now that he is dead?" "There was a time," replied Tung-mên Wu, "when I had no son, yet I never had occasion to grieve on that account. Now that my son is dead, I am only in the same condition as I was before my son was born. What reason have I, then, to mourn?"'[206] The anecdote comes from the Chinese sage Lie Yukou, known by his honorific name Liezi. What should the girl say to that? And what would go through our own heads hearing it? How can the son's 'having-been' ('Gewesen-sein') make no difference to both the times he is absent? It can only have to do with the idea that Wu is free of desire – having wished a child for himself, missing it. He will be able to be thankful for the fact that he was allowed to experience *this*; that it was a gift that he could not keep; that he cannot change the 'destiny/lot' of life – as Jullien translates the concept of *sheng-ming* – and can only comply with it, make his peace with it.[207]

That there is nothing *scandalous* about death; death is as natural as life. He is not sad, because he accepts it for what it is.[208] At the same time, it is strange for the Western reader that he compares both the phases of his son's absence in such a way. Let us recall that he does not understand them in any linear sequence – in accordance with Aristotelian physics – but instead as parallels. Thus they do not follow any hierarchy of 'time's arrow' 'forwards'. In distinction to his astonished conversation partner, however, Wu puts the emphasis on these parallels and not on the life shared with his son. His own life is thus seen from the perspective of the absolute. In this understanding there is no shift towards the Other, since both the son and the father are oriented towards the absolute, though not amongst one another any longer. (Love for the son does not have to end with his death – how else could the father consider both phases of absence to be comparable?) What alienates me in this case is that both are oriented towards the absolute and simultaneously decoupled from one another.

* * *

Relativising the self in love is sustained by desire, awakened from being affected, lives for attention to the other. Wanting to negate love, desire, and attention succeeds only in being problematically oriented towards the purportedly absolute. Desire does not reduce the Other to object when no *undertaking*, no pre-empting is considered and intended but, rather, was *opened up*, from the angle of being affected. That perspective reaches beyond our own attentiveness; it swings outwards, does not even out but, rather, is and remains excessive, worries us, sticks with us, *that* something is yet to come, an answer. *And he lifts his gaze, looks at her,* a gesture that cannot fall back on any experience when it is needed, lacks a way out, has to be trusted to be open, the gaze laid bare, without alluding, eluding, maybe the flirtation brought them this far, but now it gets serious, it is not a game any longer, he reveals that he loves her, desires her. 'A caress takes form in the contact, without this signification turning into the experience of a caress,' writes Emmanuel Levinas.[209] Experience does not peel away any touch, something is always left, only a feeling of intensity materialises, which always needs touch again, not to be extinguished, bog down, to sustain itself, on the inside and outside of physical proximity. The most intense experience leaves behind no comprehension of it, leads to its time alone, the moment of closeness, tenderness. I experience your body, not *as* body – already in this instance Levinas would also perceive the limits of the phenomenon, when no distance in the 'as' appears any longer, neither phenomenon nor experience of what is lived is left behind. Phenomenon and experience are absorbed by what happens, by coming into full effect – I can no longer remember how you looked, what your hand did with me. The self slips under consciousness, finding no repression displaced somewhere else either, *functioning* by corporeality, by shared physicality, in the soft dance of embraces, entanglements, turns, in touching skin, feeling warmth, from the body, with the body. Luce Irigaray writes: 'The caress seeks out the not yet of the female lover's blossoming. That which cannot be anticipated because it is other. The unforeseeable nature of contact with otherness, beyond its own limits. Beyond the limits of its "I can." The irreducible nature of the other's presence, which is put off to a time always in the future, which suspends parousia indefinitely.'[210] The naked skin and the naked gaze pertain to each other, confide in each other, warm themselves, give themselves, without running into any resistance. When Levinas speaks of the 'poetry of the world', then it is only in assuming 'proximity par excellence' or the 'proximity of a neighbour par excellence'.[211] From our closeness with the Other, a tenderness towards the world results, a being in love that changes our view of things. Self-relativisation in love shifts not only the notions of our own ego; it also opens our gaze in favour of a shared world.

* * *

Seen from the perspective of death, life is a question of living further or surviving. Death of the Other forms a caesura. At the same time, this 'further' comes forth in the tempo of the *'not yet'* (*'Noch-nicht'*) – it is still not time yet; it is still not our turn. Finitude is a fact. Yet what does it mean? I cannot think of my end, or of my infinity. Finitude appears to be just an irresolvable aporia. It remains therefore, as Ricœur emphasises, 'contrary to appearances (...) an abstract idea.'[212]

Surviving applies to the dead, in our living memory of them, and to the living, in our day-to-day lives, in the orienting of the lifeworld, of the world view. Two times that are constantly intermixing, from our childhoods forwards – if I think of the photograph of my great-grandfather who was a shoemaker, and who meant so much to my father who became fatherless quite early on; if I think of my grandmothers, my grandfather, my aunt who died of cancer; when I experience my parents now, experience that I myself am a father; when my daughter now experiences me the way I did with my parents at that time; and when, hopefully, she far outgrows us, up to the end of this century. An arc thus stretches from the beginning of the twentieth to the end of the twenty-first century, an arc of intimate family relationships, of physical habits, settings, stories, pictures, which we have shared and known. It is with this focus that our own remembering moves, just being remembered perhaps, as a person, not as our work and shadows.

Regarding the 'further in the tempo of the *not-yet*', Ernst Tugendhat recorded an observation, which I would once again like to take up at this juncture: 'Not until we see our fear of death as the flip-side of the will to continue living are we able to understand why we do not sense this fear from a distance. The will to continue living is always concerned with the next phase of life; it is not any will to live floating above us as such, and that is why the fear of death is also oriented towards each next phase of life.'[213] The death of the Other; the certainty of our own death do not affect the will *to live on*. In the process it becomes clear: All the effort and exertion I have cultivated in order to develop, change, convey *my memories*, *me*, and *my identity* will be taken over by nobody else in this kind of wholeness, even though everyone is entrusted, charged with this task already and only for himself. It is necessary, then, to relativise this effort and persistence already, to the benefit of a sort of equanimity that, like driftwood, carries along what would otherwise be held onto desperately. Tugendhat says: 'We could perhaps subsume this equanimity for its part under our sense of reality, because it is indicated in particular when holding on appears to be irrational, similar to the way we attempt to avoid any excess of emotions where we recognise this as incommensurate with reality, without therefore looking down on emotionality as such. In the end, that leads to the question of the desirable equilibrium between holding on and struggling, on the one hand, and letting go on the other. For it seems to be necessarily about equilibrium, after all. The austere abnegation of life, the way the Buddha taught, has as questionable an outcome as stubborn self-assertiveness. Letting go, equanimity, is moreover a stance that we wish for ourselves not only in the face of death but also in all our actions and pursuits.'[214] Death requires no *other* behaviour than what we seek for our life: The fear of death springs from the will *to live on*; we desire equanimity in all our 'doings'. How we shape the relationship between the two with each other is in the tension between reality and dealing with it appropriately. At a certain moment, the stubborn will to live becomes open to question; when hardly anyone from our own generation is still living, then we desire that equanimity for ourselves all the more. The latitude for our own possibilities, for our own acting and behaving, supports our own stance in life, which may prove to be more poignant than the question of 'identity'. In this sense, according to the philosopher Tugendhat, it is the practical questions 'we are confronted with (…): questions as to how we want to live, not questions as to how we are (…).'[215]

* * *

If death requires behaviour no different to that which applies to life, then the relationship of both to belief can be confined to that relationship between life and belief, the praxis of belief. Anthropologically, there is a lot to say for the way Tugendhat brings the relationship between will and equanimity to the fore with the question whether we can either relativise the will – in meditative exercises, for instance – or whether in accordance with the will we seek to alter the world in not accepting death and thus religiously surpassing the natural order, in notions of supernatural, miracle-working powers. As extremes of an orientation towards the absolute, neither self-abnegation nor religious revelation appear to me to be tenable ways of dealing. In this regard, I have another example in mind. The movie *Walk the line* is about the American singer Johnny Cash, whose life was deeply influenced by religious revelation.[216] The film re-enacts how as a young boy Cash lost his older brother, who fell onto a table saw and then died at home from the wound to his chest. All the dialogue in the scene is oriented towards the mindset regarding revelation: The dying boy asks his mother whether she also hears the angels, and she says yes. A child who had not grown up with the idea of revelation and its figures would certainly have put the question otherwise. Yet in any case the question would have been: What comes next? What awaits me? And here is where the impossibility of an adult attending an adult sets in, both thinking of each one's finitude. Volker Braun has shown very poignantly how adults are able to deal with it in his eulogy for Christa Wolf.[217] Yet one cannot attend the child with the answer: Here is where you life ends, *it is good the way it is*. It would be immoral – as an adult, as someone older – to tell the injustice from having grown older to the face of someone younger who trusts you, as protection, as support; and it would be immoral to degrade the still living Other as someone already destined to die, instead of assisting him, in his breathing. Morality alone, though, does not suffice in this case, to identify with the knowledge of morality and not measure up to it, after all, to see ourselves in the centre instead of the Other. The Other, the child, requires a sincere answer that does not release us from our responsibility even. There can be no betrayal, not in this situation. *I am with you*, the adult will say – just like so often at the bedside at home, in order to provide a sense of peace and comfort – *nothing can happen to you*. That will only work, though, if the words are not just said but are also believed, are proven, by the voice, its timbre, betraying no uncertainty. Being there for the child that way means believing in that consolation ourselves, no matter how much it is open to question for us. Perhaps not from being positively certain but from the determination being impossible: *I cannot think of my end, I cannot think of my infinity* – how should I argue one versus the other?

* * *

Which answer would you yourself give the girl, if you stood there with her in a picture? Which response from the year 2018? In children's books the same story is told today, about the dead bird; maybe you would show her that episode from *Pippi Longstocking*, the one where Pippi, Tommy, and Annika see a dead bird lying in the grass while on their excursion to the sea; they bury it and offer devotions for it, a moment of silence, with their kites in the air.[218] *Others also know what you have experienced*. And the child might ask: *And, how did you deal with it?* Yet would that ease her pain? At the same time, many children accept the fact that plants, animals, and people can die as a law of nature, and their indifference betrays that they do not yet relate it to themselves. In fact, it took a long time before I grew up to the idea, before I actually apprehended, understood the certainty of my own death.[219] The girl, then, can be put at ease by the thought of the immutable nature of things and, in comparing with Others, see that this is something illustrative, nothing extraordinary. Equanimity is a deciding factor in how much she trusts purported normalcy and naturalness. For she experienced uncertainty in precisely her natural capacity to trust that she would not need to worry; a bird sings and warbles. Nature is cryptic – that gives the girl cause to worry. It can turn into its opposite, become lifeless.

* * *

Little girl with dead bird is not only a picture in the permanent collection of the 'Musée Oldmasters Museum' in Brussels; along with the dove cut-out from René Magritte's *Le Retour* ('The Return', 1940) – a *modern* classic and public favourite – the *Little girl* also prominently decorates the handy museum guide to the old and new collections. In the museum shop, the motif of the girl can be bought not only on a postcard but also on the cover of a notebook. For my notes on the picture, I bought just this very booklet myself, austerely composed of cardboard, with a detail from the portrait as its cover picture. What has turned this image into the *classical* public favourite? There is no big name attached to it, no genius or old master. This picture, then, cannot serve the pop cult of celebrity in art. On the jacket of the museum guide, only the head of the girl with her ernest gaze is depicted; we recognise the old style, the realism of the portrayal – what is old does not appear in the symbolism of any distant world view but one that is closeby instead, in the figure of a girl, the way that shape was and is for all time. The fact that the picture lends itself to popularising the art of the old masters has to do with the timeless nature of its motif – from the girl's head all the way to the entire portrayal with the bird, as an anthropological motif of life and death – and with the realism of its execution. In this way, the distance of the historical is anthropologically bridged. Since popularisation requires proximity, a closeness with what is already well known, in our own time, it is no coincidence to exhibit as exemplary precisely an image that speaks to this proximity, even though it comes from a different time. In this way, the popular accessibility and understandability of art, as demanded not only from the economic but from the democratic side as well, is recouped. The image's allegory does not become overt until asking the question what would define the relationship between life and death today, what both really mean for the observer. The answer from the sixteenth century is certainly not popular today; Christian Humanism does not convey society's image of itself or of the world. Today's most popular references in the West – science-based knowledge and individualism – open the picture up to a broad yet lonely perspective, though only with a view to the solitary individual. Both the historically humanistic as well as anthropological dimension of the picture, however, go beyond this isolation. Because it has an anthropological quality, it concerns everyone – and we can make ourselves understood on the matter as a result; we are called to do so, if we ourselves intend to do justice to the claim of this quality. And even though the individual appeared with the emergence of Humanism, this was still an appeal to everyone, a social occurrence that was still far removed from thinking of *society* from the angle of the primacy of the individual, in the sense of subsequent Liberalism. We are ill prepared for the picture today: lacking more specific religious knowledge; turned into economic creatures down to our promises of good fortune; following dreams of feasibility, precisely in regard of life (eugenics) and death (euthanasia); we have to provide ourselves with an answer for the gaze of the girl, to the question what life and death mean for us. Art cannot convey the promises of religion; it only leads further into the world; yet with it, we can discuss, see, thematise what drives every one of us as human beings, how we relate to the coming and going of life. The *Little girl with dead bird* illustrates this urgency. In the concentrated form of the fragment it stands only for itself, it stands there, withstanding. And in that resisting, its popular self-evident character, the easy enjoyment of it, is transformed into an open question; and faced precisely with this question, there is no protection through historical distance; once again, it is the anthropology of images that does not let go of the observer. He was lured in by it, yet its power takes hold of him inexorably. Everything appeared to be so easily surveyed, so comprehensible – yet nothing is explained from what can be seen. The simplicity is revealed to be a riddle – what is the gaze telling us?

* * *

A volume of poetry by Wisława Szymborska has been translated into German as *Deshalb leben wir* ('Why we live').[220] What does she tell us? Scattered in the volumes of her poetry, we find quiet gestures;

here and there I have already mentioned them: 'The joy of writing./The power of preserving.' And unable to decide, cutting both ways: 'Revenge of a mortal hand.'[221] (For does the hand know how to avenge; does mortality avenge itself?) In another passage she writes, 'Day to day I trust in permanence,/in history's prospects.'[222] And again: 'The world is never ready/for the birth of a child.//(...) can we begin anew.'[223] Life and death are not a circle, of course, that closes, concludes – our own actions unfold, make circles, extend into new situations. We can be relativised *sideways* yet our own traces and actions also have a sideways effect, are differentiated, pass away, go over into something Other. It is necessary to see both sorts of relativisations, effects. Or as Szymborska said in her speech accepting the Nobel Prize in Literature in 1996: 'I sometimes dream of situations that can't possibly come true. I audaciously imagine, for example, that I get a chance to chat with the Ecclesiastes, the author of that moving lament on the vanity of all human endeavors. I would bow very deeply before him, because he is, after all, one of the greatest poets, for me at least. That done, I would grab his hand. " 'There's nothing new under the sun': that's what you wrote, Ecclesiastes. But you yourself were born new under the sun. And the poem you created is also new under the sun, since no one wrote it down before you. And all your readers are also new under the sun, since those who lived before you couldn't read your poem."'[224] What is new blocks the way of things, does not comply, branches off, gets lost. It is fleeting, but only in this fleeting condition does it develop its own quality. Birth and death are not any standard dimensions with which we can build metaphysically. Only in acting, speaking can what is new be found, uttered, shown over and over again, just as Hannah Arendt spoke of it. And this present time of doing cannot become undone, once it has happened. It can pass away – because it was there. Therein lies the paradox of forgetting: Only because the present took place does forgetting follow it. Forgetting does not extinguish what was. It leaves behind what was. Nothing says that it is unable to become visible again under new conditions, otherwise. Yet that is revealed only in present times to come, without any guarantee. Scattered, forsaken, what remains, what was. Nothing personal, for certain – a stone, a shard, paths we did not go down, words we understood how to form, how others form them and are able to read them. 'And whatever I do', the poetess writes, 'will become forever what I've done.'[225] That is how we live our lives away, by our own power, as a result of what comes into being with it.

* * *

Why we live requires a completely different answer, though. In what regard is our own humanity made manifest? Is not loving, and being loved, that very quality in which both the young and the old find their humanity?[226] And would it not be this experience that proves the quality of our lives, rather than measuring their value in years? An experience in and of itself to which nothing can be added, which is singular, which constitutes the profundity of what I, as a human being, am able to experience in life, the core of what I am able to achieve? For our lives can only be about what is qualitative, not about the scale (being remembered, being well known), which always gets lost in the immeasurability of time and space. Being supported by this experience is what would be good. (And that is how it is in Szymborska, after all: 'But it just so happens that I am with you./And I really see nothing/ordinary about it.'[227])

* * *

The stiff composition of the picture, the build of the small girl, the slight turning of the whole body with her head, in the direction of her gaze, these things are contrasted with the colour sections, which in no way observe the line of representation but are layered on top of one another and are shifting, the way the light blue of the collar goes into the garment, the way the delicate red lightens her cheeks, the way the shadows (subsequently intensified) lie upon her temple, coming down from the reddish hairline. It is a healthy girl there, looking out, a small, vigorous girl. Only her hand is covered by gray, the red just weakly shimmering through, the pink. And whereas the shadow under her left breast is purely pictorial, flat, blurred, the shadows on her right upper arm, on the sleeve, have been carefully worked out in every fold. In the same subject, the portrayal of shadows, the tactile and the pictorial qualities are closest together. And then the yellowish, brownish shimmering sleeve, the garment, the bonnet, a weak lustre to the plain clothing, suggesting the affluence this child knew only in the half-rings, almost appearing golden, for the laces on her breast. What might the painter himself have spoken with the child about why she should be depicted in this way? The picture does not remain in its frame, the gaze of the child opens its framework up into our space, without the self-assured severity of direct eye contact, the way Cranach or Dürer painted it, yet instead indirect; we cannot see what the girl sees, though perhaps she does not see it herself, either; she just looks, questioning and uncertain. We are not at all able to apprehend directly the relationship between life and death, as of we could comprehend both, within the framework of exemplary tales. There is no tragedy being illustrated here, only a question being posed, silently and speechlessly. And the dark background also poses it, also raises it, taking it into our space, here where only the answer can be. Whether the girl saw her picture as an older woman? Perhaps, if she was the daughter of the painter.

My observation on the image, my essay has run its course, having described in detail the picture itself, explored its art-historical connections, gone into its effects above and beyond the historical era. Through investigating one impact of the intercultural everyday life in contemporary museum visits, the alignment of the history of art and the anthropology of images became significant – an alignment that, with regard for the anthropology of images, had to answer the question of art and, with regard for historicity, the question of human destinies, in life and death. Moreover, an allegory of life and death asks for an interpretation of its subject, an interpretation that has to be proven historically as well as interculturally, and which requires philosophical comment as to how this topic can indeed be treated today. Against the historical backdrop, the question of belief emerged, in relationship to life and death. With the aid of philosophical readings, I have attempted to treat that question, always with a view to my own particular answer for it. For in the end the challenge coming from the picture – what answer do you give? – should be taken seriously. In the vast field of considerations, I have marked out my own stopping points, preferences in orienting the precarious relationship between belief, life, and death. In its impressive aesthetic, the picture made it possible to contemplate this ethical orientation. It opens itself up, reveals itself, yet does not take any position, offer any recogniseable interpretation, or move within any familiar symbolism. Catullus appeared to be one possible iconographic source, and iconology would select Humanism as the context for its interpretability. However, the picture's tension, its 'iconic' interpretation – to use the Max Imdahl's way of observing – arises from its entire countenance and physical stance, with which the child's question is expressed, a question that she herself cannot yet even formulate; she does not stir, stiffens, only looks upwards, into the distance. The child lacks the reference points, and the work in the answer is to give those markers to her. That is the work of observers and, as they soon determine, it means working on themselves as well, for which answer should we give? An answer that we believe, one that does not come easily, which takes the question seriously, makes it clearly resound, all the way to our own core. What does life mean, what does death mean?

'Campo S. Polo. The old man over on the next bench, on whose hand a sparrow sits, chirping, allowing itself to be petted. One bench further, the blonde girl writing something in a notebook; and the little boys playing football, intermittently stepping up to the iron fountain, making their hair soaking wet and going back to the game with the gravitas of a professional. When I move on, the boys are gone, the girl has filled an entire page, and from the old man's hand there's still that delicate chirping.'

Harald Hartung,
from chronicles recorded in:
Der Tag vor dem Abend (Göttingen, 2012)

Written the summer of 2011 to the summer of 2013,
for Hanna

Notes

1. Cf. Erwin Panofsky, *Meaning in the Visual Arts* (New York, 1955), as well as his *Aufsätze zu Grundfragen der Kunstwissenschaft* (Berlin, 1985) and, in addition, Max Imdahl, *Giotto – Arenafresken. Ikonographie, Ikonologie, Ikonik* (Munich, 1996), Chapter VIII, "Ikonographie – Ikonologie – Ikonik".
2. In 2007, for example, it was part of an extensive show of Flemish and Chinese art in Brussels' Palais des Beaux-Arts, curated by Luc Tuymans and Yu Hui, where works by Jan van Eyck, Petrus Christus or Jan Brueghel the Elder were shown in contrast to those by Chen Lu, Zhu Jianshen, Shen Zhou and others. (cf. the exhibition catalogue *L'Empire interdit – Visions du monde des maîtres chinois et flamands* [Brussels, 2007])
3. Cf. Hans Belting, *The End of the history of art?* (Chicago, 1987) as well as his *Anthropology of images: Picture, medium, body* (Princeton, 2011)
4. Max Imdahl, *Giotto – Arenafresken*, op. cit., p. 97
5. Cf. ibid., p. 92
6. E-mail from Joost Vander Auwera to the author, dated 28 June 2013: The picture was 'given to the museum by the family of a young soldier who had died on the battlefied during the First World War' (in the original Dutch: '(...) is het geschonken door de familie van een jonge soldaat die tijdens de eerste wereldoorlog op het slagveld is gestorven').
7. Cited in Katlijne Van der Stighelen, *Hoofd en bijzaak – Portretkunst in Vlaanderen van 1420 tot nu* (Leuven, 2008), p. 61
8. Cited by Anton Korteweg, "With a Poet's Eye – A Few Dutch Poems on Dutch Paintings", in: *The Low Countries – Arts and Society in Flanders and the Netherlands*, RNS 1103, No. 19 (Rekkem; Raamsdonksveer, 2011)
9. Cf. *Pride and joy. Children's portraits in the Netherlands 1500-1700*, ed. J. B. Bedaux and R. Ekkart, (Ghent; Amsterdam, 2000), and *Kinderen op hun mooist. Het kinderportret in de Nederlanden 1500-1700*, ed. J. B. Bedaux and R. Ekkart, (Ghent; Amsterdam, 2000)

10. Lauran Toorians, "Portrait of the Child as Sitter – *Children of a Golden Age*," in: *The Low Countries – Arts and Society in Flanders and the Netherlands*, Stichting Ons Erfdeel (Rekkem; Raamsdonksveer, 2001), p. 185
11. Ibid., p. 188. In 1592, the sixteenth-century Flemish humanist Justus Lipsius wrote to a friend after the death of the friend's child: 'Life is like a bird that a child holds in its hands. It often flies away while still very young' (cited in Patrick De Rynck, *Dit is België – In tachtig meesterwerken*, [Amsterdam, 2010], p. 66). In this case, the bird is alive in symbolising the death of a child – not dead as in the case of the *Little girl with dead bird*.
12. Leo Van Puyvelde, "L'enfant à l'oiseau mort – Un portrait de Marguerite d'Autriche par Juan de Flandres", in: *Les Arts Plastiques*, No. 7-8 (Brussels, 1948), p. 267 (in the original French: 'J'ai passé vingt ans près de ce tableau, effigie toute simple d'une enfant de trois ans qui, d'un air triste, tient dans ses petites mains un oiseau mort. Jamais je n'ai pu regarder ce visage sans retrouver l'émotion si douce, si sincère, qu'éprouve tout visiteur des Musées de Bruxelles dès le premier contact lors-qu'il s'arrête devant cette œuvre à la fois charmante et profonde.')
13. Ibid. (in the original French: 'Ce qui fait la valeur de ce tableau, c'est la physionomie toute éclairée de vie intérieure et la pudeur de ce sentiment de tristesse si délicatement exprimé; ce sont avant tout les moyens techniques dont l'artiste s'est servi pour exprimer son émotion.')
14. Leo Van Puyvelde, "L'enfant à l'oiseau mort" (in the original French: 'avec la netteté d'un buste sculpté')
15. Cf. Heinrich Wölfflin, *Principles of art history. The Problem of the development of style in later art*, (New York, 1932), Chapter I, "Linear and Painterly", pp. 56f.
16. Letter from Ludwig Burchard to Leo Van Puyvelde, dated 20 November 1931, contained in the file on the painting under its inventory number 4434, in the archive of the Royal Museums of Fine Arts in Brussels (in the original German: 'Ich zeigte das Photo [des Gemäldes] kürzlich Dr. Friedländer. (...) Er würde es sehr begrüssen, wenn dieses Bildnis, das ihn immer lebhaft interessiert habe, gereinigt würde.').
17. Ibid.
18. Leo Van Puyvelde, "L'application de la radiographie aux tableaux", in: *Journal de radiologie et d'électrologie*, Paris, Volume XVII, No. 2

(February, 1933), p. 90 (the two citations in the original French: '(...) vous avez bien vu, le fond a été jadis d'un vert clair je crois, mais je n'ai pu encore examiner à fond si c'était du vert-de-gris. Il est très visible encore sous la battée du cadre; ce vert a été couvert d'une couleur brunâtre très opaque (...).' and 'Sur le front de l'enfant se trouve une couleur grisâtre que je crois être due à une restauration; peut-être, me disais-je, les rayons × décèleront-ils d'autres repeints. J'ai fait radiographier le tableau. Sur la radiographie le repeint récent ne projette aucune ombre. Et la radiographie décèle quelques reprises. L'examen visuel démontre que ces reprises sont faites dans la même pâte que le reste, et qu'elles sont toutes des améliorations. Ce ne sont pas des repeints à enlever; ce sont des repentirs de l'artiste, qui travaillait lentement, qui se corrigeait lui-même.')

19. Cf. Matthias Weniger, *Sittow, Morros, Juan de Flandes – Drei Maler aus dem Norden am Hof Isabellas der Katholischen* (Kiel, 2011), p. 381
20. Leo Van Puyvelde, "L'enfant à l'oiseau mort", op. cit., p. 268 (in the original French: 'A cette époque, seuls les enfants princiers bénéficiaient d'un pareil honneur.')
21. Ibid., p. 269
22. *Alte Meister – 1300-1800 im Städel Museum*, exhibition catalogue (Frankfurt; Ostfildern, 2011), p. 78 (in the original German: 'Der vierjährige Ruprecht spielt Falkner – allerdings mit einem Spatzen, der auf seinem Falknerhandschuh sitzt!')
23. Cf. *Les Arts Plastiques* (Brussels, 1949), pp. 227-231, under the heading "Notes et commentaires"
24. Recently, Dagmar Eichberger and Katlijne Van der Stighelen have suggested the painter Michael Sittow as the picture's author; Matthias Weniger disputes this attribution (cf. Dagmar Eichberger, *Leben mit Kunst, Wirken durch Kunst – Sammelwesen und Hofkunst unter Margarete von Österreich, Regentin der Niederlande* [Turnhout, 2002], p. 396; Katlijne Van der Stighelen, *Hoofd en bijzaak*, op. cit., p. 59; and Matthias Weniger, op. cit., pp. 381-382)
25. The letter is found in the archival file for the portrait at the Museums of Fine Arts in Brussels (No. 4434). The original there reads: 'L'examen aux rayons × a permis de constater que: Il y a beaucoup de surpeints qui donnent du vague à nombre d'éléments qui subsistent, plus nets, sous ces surpeints. Ce sont notamment: une ombre portée sur le fond qui est presque entièrement voilée, un décor très net sur la ceinture qui n'est presque plus visible, le menton est plus allongé qu'il ne parait actuellement, les yeux sont plus nets qu'on ne le voit

actuellement, le volume est plus accusé, la bouche présente elle aussi des surpeints, le fond vert est très surpeint.'
26. Cf. note 18 above. The original text of the letter (with the same source information as in note 25 above) reads: 'Légère usure, notamment dans les ombres, accompagné par endroits de nombreuses mais très petites lacunes entre autre sur la main droite. Griffe étroite à droite de l'œil droit: griffe plus large sous l'épaule gauche: chaîne de lacunes à droite du corsage et à la face intérieure du bras droit. Surpeint léger des ombres. Restauration de l'aile gauche du nez et au milieu de la lèvre supérieure surpeinte sur la droite: trois masticages forment taches sur le décolleté et l'épaule droite: restauration plus importante du fond au coin droit inférieur. Surpeint ancien ou modification de l'iris de l'œil droit. La radiographie révèle une ombre réservée sur le fond au-dessus de l'épaule droite et une modification de la forme du cou et des épaules par rapport au contour initial du fond bleu qui marque nettement un repentir sur l'épaule gauche. Le fond vert, composé de deux ou trois couches à base de vert-de-gris et d'huile siccative, recouvre une couche bleue composée d'azurite, d'ocre, de blanc de plomb et d'huile siccative. L'absence d'exsudation sur le bleu exclut la possibilité d'une modification peu après le séchage de la matière bleue. L'absence d'interprénetration des matières vertes et bleues rend l'hypothèse de l'exécution originale peu vraisemblable. L'absence de couche intermédiaire et le dégagement des pigments à la surface de la couche bleue fait penser à un fond bleu qui aurait été nettoyé puis surpeint de vert. Les stries brunes, parallèles, qui marquent l'ombre du bonnet seraient des touches de blaireautage. Certaines de ces touches auraient été arrêtées par l'application d'un écran rectiligne posé sur la peinture.'
27. Cf. D. Shawe-Taylor; J. Scott, *Brueghel to Rubens – Masters of Flemish Painting* (London, 2007), p. 62
28. Cf. Victor I. Stoichita, *The Self-Aware Image. An Insight Into Early Modern Meta-Painting* (Turnhout, 2015)
29. *De brieven van Rubens*, ed. L. Huet (Amsterdam, 2006), pp. 26-27 (in the original Dutch: '(...) de schilderijen, die ik met eigen handen zo voorzichtig mogelijk heb geschikt en ingepakt (...), bleken vandaag in het huis van heer Hannibal Iberti rot en aangevreten te zijn, zo zeer dat ik bijna wanhoop ze te kunnen herstellen.')
30. Bob Claessens, "Fillette à l'oiseau mort", in: *Peinture vivante*, 6, Cultura ed. (Brussels, 1968-1969), 6/38 (in the original French:

'La Renaissance, en invitant l'homme à réfléchir aux problèmes de la vie terrestre avec l'acuité que le Moyen Age apportait à ceux de la vie future, en mettant l'accent sur l'individualisme et la dignité humaine a tout naturellement, en peinture, mis l'accent sur la technique et l'art du portrait. (...) Le portrait individuel, indépendant de tout thème chrétien devait bientôt séduire Van Eyck. (...) nous considérons la *Fillette à l'oiseau mort*, œuvre, qui elle aussi se situe aux premières années de la Renaissance (...). Nous ne connaissons aucune autre œuvre, datant de cette époque, où les sentiments du personnage représenté – chagrin, surprise, pleurs – soient ainsi étalés en public (sauf dans les tableaux religieux, bien entendu). Cette émotion du peintre et de son modèle, ainsi que l'adjonction du frêle cadavre que l'enfant tient entre ses mains, font de ce panneau un "tableau de genre", genre bien ignoré à l'epoque. (...) Certes, le problème de la mort a préoccupé les peintres de la Renaissance, mais pour la première fois, dans l'histoire de la peinture, c'est un enfant qui se trouve confronté avec le problème et cela donne à ce tableau (...) une résonnance particulièrement douloureuse et profonde.')

31. Patrick De Rynck, *Dit is België*, op. cit.
32. Anne-Marie Legaré also poses this question in her discussion of the picture for the exhibition catalogue *Women of Distinction. Margaret of York/Margaret of Austria*, in which she states: 'Perhaps it alludes to the ancient genre of mourning dead animals. Catullus, for example, recalls the pain experienced by his beloved upon the death of her sparrow.' See *Women of Distinction. Margaret of York/Margaret of Austria*, exhibition catalogue Mechelen Lamot, ed. D. Eichberger (Leuven, 2005), p. 139. Jan Baptist Bedaux also draws attention to this reference, in: *Kinderen op hun mooist*, p. 88.
33. Cf. Ovid, *Metamorphoses*, trans. Charles Martin (New York, 2004), p. 272, as well as the painting *The Fall of Icarus* in the Brussels Museum of Fine Arts. It was attributed to Pieter Bruegel (the Elder), yet according to current investigation the painting was only created after his death in 1569 – possibly as a copy of a lost original, in the way copies were regularly produced in workshops at that time. (As to the spelling of the surname, it should be noted that Pieter Bruegel was the only one to write his family name without the 'h', though the sons in his atelier wrote it with the 'h'. In these respects, I am speaking of the Brueghels' workshop as a whole, and of Pieter Bruegel the Elder in particular.) The practice of making copies in the workshop was presented very vividly in the exhibition *De Firma Brueghel*

in Maastricht and Brussels in 2002; see the exhibition catalogue *De Firma Brueghel*, P. v. d. Brink, ed. (Ghent; Amsterdam, 2002). Much as the anonymous *Little girl with dead bird* in Brussels has inspired this essay's observations, so too Bruegel's *Fall of Icarus* served as a source of earlier meditations on life and death. Thus, in W.H. Auden's "Musée des Beaux Arts" (1940), we read: 'About suffering they were never wrong,/The Old Masters: how well they understood/Its human position; how it takes place/While someone else is eating or opening a window or just walking dully along; (...)//In Breughel's Icarus, for instance: how everything turns away/Quite leisurely from the disaster; the ploughman may/Have heard the splash, the forsaken cry,/But for him it was not an important failure; the sun shone/As it had to on the white legs disappearing into the green/Water; and the expensive delicate ship that must have seen/Something amazing, a boy falling out of the sky,/Had somewhere to get to and sailed calmly on.'

34. This translation of "Poem 5", Catullus' ode to Lesbia, by Charles Martin, in his *Catullus* (New Haven, 1992), pp. 51-52

35. Cf. David Mannings, *Sir Joshua Reynolds – A Complete catalogue of his paintings* (New Haven; London, 2000), 'Plates', p. 603 and 'Text', p. 543

36. Cf. Eddy De Jongh, "Erotica in vogelperspectief – De dubbelzinnigheid van een reeks 17de eeuwse genrevoorstellingen", in: *Simiolus, Kunsthistorisch tijdschrift*, Vol. 3 (1968-69), pp. 48-49

37. Cf. ibid. In the case of Justus Lipsius at the end of the sixteenth century, a child's escaped bird was understood to be a metaphor for the child's death (cf. note 11 above). How does the erotic connotation in the case of van Mieris relate to this? Here there is a comparable tension between the allegory for death and erotic representation as there is between the *Little girl with dead bird* in Brussels and the later erotic genre paintings with the same name. In terms of depth psychology, the permeation of these orientations points not least of all to an historically revealed set of problems in dealing with life and death, eros and thanatos.

38. Cf. Jean-Baptiste Greuze's 1765 picture (Ill. 7) in the collection of Scottish National Portrait Gallery, which shows a canary. In *The Harz journey* (1824), Heinrich Heine reports of a girl from the German town Halle 'who was in love with a student. When the latter left Halle, she no longer spoke to anyone, ate little, wept day and night, and kept looking at the canary which her lover had once given

her. "The bird died, and soon after that Lore died too!" was the end of the story (...)' (Heinrich Heine, in: *The Harz journey and selected prose*, trans. R. Robertson, [London, 1993], p. 74). Did Heine know Greuze's picture – personally, from a copy, or from the discussion dedicated to it in Denis Diderot's salon? – and/or was it painted after a well-known topos, the scheme for which Heine also utilised, in his portrayal of "Lore from Halle"? The erotic motif is transferred here into one of death. In this context, cf. the way both motifs overlap in regard of the *Little girl with dead bird* in Brussels and the erotic genre of the same name as well as that of the motif of the esaped bird as a metaphor for death – in the case of Lipsius – and as an erotic allusion in the case of van Mieris. – Around 1800, Greuze turned once again to the subject *Little girl with dead bird*, though now with the portrayal of curiosity. *Un enfant hésitant àutoucher un oiseau dans la crainte qu'il soit mort, dit l'oiseau mort* (oil on panel, with the dimensions 68 × 55 cm, R.F. 1523) shows a girl as curious as she is hesitant, opening with the fingers of her right hand the right wing of a bird lying on its back, obviously dead. In this instance, neither grief nor melancholy are foregrounded but, rather – to borrow the phrase from Søren Kierkegaard – the *pleasing anxiousness* of curiosity (cf. Søren Kierkegaard, *The Concept of anxiety*, ed. and trans. Reidar Thomte [Princeton, 1980], p. 42, where one reads: 'The anxiety that is posited in innocence is (...) no suffering (...). In observing children, one will discover this anxiety intimated more particularly as a seeking for the adventurous, the monstrous, and the enigmatic. (...) This anxiety belongs so essentially to a child that he cannot do without it. Though it causes him anxiety, it captivates him by its pleasing anxiousness.')

39. Cf. Eddy De Jongh, op. cit., pp. 43-48
40. In the nineteenth century, such representations are found in Anselm Feuerbach (1854) and in the Danish sculptor Jens Adolf Jerichau (1871). These works are likewise based on this thematic history, though they interpret it in accordance with their times. In that regard, additional shifts result (removed from the tradition that lasted until the Sentimentalist stories of the eighteenth century), which I prefer not to go into here in any detail, since they do not allow for any further conclusions to be drawn for our sixteenth-century picture in Brussels. Feuerbach's portrait can be found in Hanover's Lower Saxony State Museum (Niedersächsisches Landesmuseum

Hannover) and Jerichau's sculpture in Copenhagen's Ny Carlsberg Glyptotek.
41. Cf. Catullus, "Poem 3", in: Charles Martin, *Catullus* (New Haven, 1992), pp. 50-51
42. Ibid., p. 51
43. That was how Gotthold Ephraim Lessing put it, in regard of the Ancient Greek sculpture of Laocoön and his sons: 'The master strove to attain the highest beauty possible under the given condition of physical pain. The demands of beauty could not be reconciled with the pain in all its disfiguring violence, so it had to be reduced. The scream had to be softened to a sigh, not because screaming betrays an ignoble soul, but because it distorts the features in a disgusting manner.' (Gotthold Ephraim Lessing, *Laocoön: An Essay on the limits of painting and poetry*, trans. E. A. McCormick [Baltimore, 1984], p. 17)
44. On this still unsettled debate, see note 24 above.
45. Matthias Weniger, *Sittow, Morros, Juan de Flandes* (Kiel, 2011), p. 382 (in the original German: 'Der mit großer Meisterschaft gemalte Spatz gehört zum alten Bestand (…). Die genrehafte Thematik wurde spätestens im Lauf des Malprozesses eingeführt. Zusammen mit der außerordentlich modernen Auffassung, Anlage und Proportionierung des Bildnisses und der Mode weist sie mit Nachdruck in das 16. Jahrhundert. Das Kostüm und namentlich die Form des Dekolletés deuten auf eine Entstehung nicht vor dessen zweitem Jahrzehnt (…).')
46. Cf. Bob Claessens, "Fillette à l'oiseau mort", op. cit.
47. Matthias Weniger, *Sittow, Morros, Juan de Flandes*, op. cit. (in the original German: 'So weisen die maltechnisch besonders auffälligen tiefen, subtil abgestuften Schatten an Schläfe und Mieder ebenso Übermalungen oder zumindest Verstärkungen auf wie die von einer ähnlichen Feinheit der Modellierung geprägten Hände. Auch die für die Gesamtwirkung und den berühmten Blick (…) so entscheidenden Iris und Pupillen sind überarbeitet. Schultern und Halskontur wurden nachträglich verändert. Mit dieser Maßnahme und einer Neugestaltung des Hintergrunds hängen sinnentstellende Übermalungen an der Haube des Mädchens zusammen. Der – wie heute noch an der Stirn – transparente Tüll hatte links und rechts unten die alte Hintergrundfarbe durchscheinen lassen. Der schon mit bloßem Auge zu erahnende alte Verlauf harmoniert mit der tieferen, ursprünglichen Schulterlinie.')

48. Cf. the presentation "Quelques observations faites le 14/11/94 avec M. Weniger" by Pascale Syfer-d'Olne, dated 10 January 1995. In it, under the title "Modifications et restaurations au niveau de la couche picturale", she writes on the results of the radiography: 'L'observation de la radiographie et de la photo IR (L 12246 B) révèle qu'il y a eu des modifications dans la forme des épaules, du cou et du bonnet: les épaules et le décolleté étaient situés plus bas, tandis que deux pans du bonnet se réjoignaient sous le menton (…). Les modifications qui furent apportées ne relèvent probablement pas de reprises de forme originales, exécutées lors de la création de l'œuvre, mais sont, sans doute, contemporaines de l'application du fond vert dont le rapport de R. Sneyers (IRPA, 21 mars 1966) nous dit qu'il dort s'agir d'un surpeint posé sur le fond original de teinte bleue. Effectivement, ce surpeint vert recouvre les bords du bonnet, le long des joues, et c'est peut-être pour éviter un effet d'allongement du cou (…) que l'on a en même temps rehaussé les épaules et le bord du décolleté. Ces transformations sont fort probablement dues au mauvais état de la peinture: autant la fillette que son costume montrent des traces avancées d'usure. Cette altération est sans doute causée par l'usage de solvants trop puissants lors d'un dévernissage ancien. On a tenté d'attéruer ces traces d'usure dans les ombres en posant un glacis foncé (…). La radiographie montre aussi la présence de diverses petites lacunes et de griffes. Le ton bleu situé sous le fond vert est visible le long du bord droit du panneau (…).' (Pascale Syfer-d'Olne, "Quelques observations faites le 14/11/94 avec M. Weniger", archive file no. 4434 of the Royal Museums of Fine Arts, Brussels). Supplementing the report by Sneyers, it includes, in particular, the assumption that the overpainting was possibly undertaken on account of the poor state of the picture, which is documented by the wear and tear shown on the dress portrayed. Whether at an 'earlier' or 'more recent' time is not acknowledged.
49. Matthias Weniger, *Sittow, Morros, Juan de Flandes*, op. cit. (in the original German: 'Ohne die nachträgliche Akzentuierung der Schatten würde das Gemälde vermutlich noch jünger wirken' and 'schon vor den Übermalungen äußerst sanften Übergänge. Kaum merklich löst sich das helle Rosa der unteren Lippe in den umgebenden Inkarnatston auf'.)
50. Philippe Forest, *Tous les enfants sauf un* (Paris, 2007), p. 93 (in the original French: 'La mort est l'aporie majeure devant laquelle

défaille tout système symbolique et en réponse à laquelle il se constitue.')

51. Cf. Hans Blumenberg, *Ästhetische und metaphorologische Schriften* (Frankfurt, 2001), p. 262: 'Unsere Erkenntnis ist ihrem Wesen nach schon Kunst und Technik in eins, *die* "ars humana", die sich erst sekundär aufspaltet in die Ausdrucks- und Werkformen der "Kunst" und "Technik" im neuzeitlichen Sinne. Erstmals zeigt sich die menschliche *Autonomie* als der Grundzug der heraufziehenden Epoche; aber ihr Ursprung ist (...) die Antwort auf die Not der wesenhaften Fremdheit in dieser Welt (...).'
52. Paul Ricœur, *Living up to death*, trans. David Pellauer (Chicago, 2009), p. 59
53. Ibid., p. 76
54. Cf. Renate Berger, *Rodolfo Valentino – Biografie* (Hamburg, 2003)
55. Cf. Hans Blumenberg, *Lebenszeit und Weltzeit* (Frankfurt, 2001), p. 83, where one reads: 'Institutionen beruhen gerade darauf, daß die Lebenszeit nicht das Maß aller Dinge ist, vielmehr Verfügungen über deren Grenzen hinaus getroffen, Traditionen über sie hinweg gesetzt und angenommen werden müssen.'
56. Philippe Forest, op. cit., p. 83 (in the original French: 'Il y a quelque chose d'universel dans la condition humaine qui tient à ce que celle-ci est partout et toujours, par le désir et par le deuil, confrontation avec l'impossible réel. Et la mort de l'enfant est l'une des figures de cet impossible.')
57. Wisława Szymborska, "Into the ark" in: *Poems, new and collected, 1957–1997*, trans. Stanislaw Baranczak and Claire Cavanagh (New York, 1998), pp. 212f.
58. Jacob and Wilhelm Grimm, "The Companionship of cat and mouse" ("Katze und Maus in Gesellschaft"), in: *The Original folk and fairy tales of the Brothers Grimm*, trans. and ed. Jack Zipes, reprint (Princeton, 2016), p. 16
59. Ibid., p. 17
60. Jacob and Wilhelm Grimm, "Katze und Maus in Gesellschaft", in: *Das große deutsche Märchenbuch*, ed. H. Brackert (Munich; Zürich, 1994), p. 134 (the orginal German: '[S]o geht's in der Welt.')
61. Theodor W. Adorno, *Aesthetic theory*, trans. Robert Hullot-Kentor (London, 1997), p. 245
62. Rudolf Boehm, *Grundriß einer Poietik* (Würzburg, 2005), p. 12 (in the original German: '[Hoffen] dürfen wir nur, imstande zu sein,´

NOTES 153

einzusehen, was wir wissen müssen, zu begreifen, was wir tun sollten, und zu bewerkstelligen, was wir machen können.')
63. Emmanuel Levinas, *Time and the other*, trans. Richard A. Cohen (Pittsburgh, 1987), p. 69
64. Paul Ricœur, *Living up to death*, op. cit., p. 85
65. Ibid.; n.b.: the parentheses have been inserted by Catherine Goldenstein and Jean-Louis Schlegel, the French publishers of the fragments, which appeared posthumously.
66. Paul Ricœur, *Memory, history, forgetting*, trans. Kathleen Blamey and David Pellauer (Chicago, 2004), pp. 442f. The study cites from Jankélévitch as an epigraph: 'He who has been, from then on cannot have been: henceforth this mysterious and profoundly obscure fact of having been is his viaticum for all eternity.' In Jankélévitch's treatise *Der Tod* (originally published in French as *La mort* [Paris, 1966]), this idea is found as a basic theme in many places, as in the following passage: 'Dieses Gewesen-sein ist wie das Gespenst eines unbekannten kleinen Mädchens, das in Auschwitz gefoltert und ermordet wurde: eine Welt, in der der flüchtige Aufenthalt dieses Kindes auf Erden stattgefunden hat, wird sich auf immer und unwiderruflich von einer Welt unterscheiden, in der dieser Aufenthalt nicht stattgefunden hat. Was gewesen ist, kann nicht nicht gewesen sein.' (Cf. Vladimir Jankélévitch, *Der Tod* [Frankfurt, 2005], p. 560 and, furthermore, p. 207 and pp. 551–552)
67. Paul Ricœur, *Living up to death*, p. 86
68. Ibid.
69. Ibid.
70. Primo Levi, "In the park", in: *A Tranquil star: Unpublished stories of Primo Levi*, trans. and ed. Ann Goldstein and Alessandra Bastagli (New York, 2007), p. 71
71. Rudolf Boehm, *Kritik der Grundlagen des Zeitalters* (The Hague, 1974); this foreword has no page numbers and is dated 24 September 1973 (in the original German: 'Aber am Ende ist überhaupt mit dem Verlust von Hoffnungen und Erwartungen gar nichts verloren, nur die Freiheit zurückgewonnen. Denn nichts Gutes oder Nützliches ist, was uns Menschen betrifft, zu erhoffen oder zu erwarten; es ist nur zu tun und zu besorgen.')
72. Rudolf Boehm, *Grundriß einer Poietik*, op. cit. (in the original German: 'Und was ist es denn, was wir wissen müssen?'; and 'Wenn ich diese Frage hier in nur zwei Worten beantworten soll, kann ich nur sagen: Wir müssen begreifen, daß die un-menschliche Natur

nicht eben menschenfreundlich ist (...). Das Weltall (...) ist offenbar sogar lebensfeindlich, bis hin zu den uns benachbarten Planeten, mit denen wir eine gemeinsame Sonne teilen. Aber auch unsere lebensfreudige Erde hat nicht nur die Natur menschenfreundlicher Berge und Täler, Flüsse und Seen, Wälder, Felder und Wiesen, sondern auch die stürmischer Meere, glühender Wüsten, eiskalter Steppen und unwegsamer Gebirge und überhaupt unwirtlicher Witterungen.')

73. In 2010, I was a guest in Boehm's philosophical discussion group at Ghent University, in which vehement debates included Jürgen Habermas' shift from post-metaphysical to post-secular thought, that is, the question whether religion can serve also as a source of inspiration for philosophical considerations.

74. Friedrich Nietzsche, *The Antichrist*, trans. Walter Kaufmann, in: *The Portable Nietzsche*, ed. Walter Kaufmann (New York, 1976), pp. 581f.

75. Cf. Emmanuel Levinas, *Time and the other*, p. 71. This idea is found not only in Epicurus' *Letter to Menoeceus* but similarly in Epictetus' *Enchiridion*, in Lucretius, and in Prodicus (see Diogenes Laërtius, *Lives and opinions of eminent philosophers*, trans. R. D. Hicks [Cambridge, MA, 1925]; as well as Theodor Gomperz, *Greek thinkers: A History of ancient philosophy*, 3 vols., trans. L. Magnus and G. Berry [New York, 1905])

76. Maurice Merleau-Ponty, *The Visible and the invisible*, ed. C. Lefort, trans. A. Lingis (Evanston, 1968), pp. 84f.

77. Vladimir Jankélévitch notes: "Der Tod der Eltern (...) hebt die Vermittlung zwischen dem Tod in der dritten Person und dem eigenen Tod auf; das (...) Glacis, das das Konzept des Todes von unserem persönlichen Tod getrennt hatte, ist gefallen (...)." (Vladimir Jankélévitch, *Der Tod*, op. cit., p. 40)

78. Cf. Lars Gustafsson: 'Was wir intuitiv "Leben" nennen, das heißt Organismen mit Körperteilen und dem Vermögen, sich fortzubewegen, entsteht erst explosionsartig im Kambrium, vor 500 Millionen Jahren.' In: Lars Gustafsson, *Gegen Null – Eine mathematische Phantasie* (Zurich, 2011), p. 29

79. Ernst Tugendhat, *Anthropologie statt Metaphysik* ('Anthropology instead of metaphysics') (Munich, 2010), p. 191 (in the original German: 'daß einerseits das Bedürfnis nach einem Götterglauben nicht nur ein kulturelles, sondern ein anthropologisches, in der Struktur des menschlichen Seins begründetes Phänomen ist, daß es

NOTES

aber für den heutigen Menschen, wenn er sich nichts vormacht, unmöglich ist, diesem Bedürfnis nachzugeben.')

80. Rudolf Boehm, *Kritik der Grundlagen des Zeitalters*, op. cit., pp. 71-72 (in the original German: 'Sie ist eine Erlösungslehre. Erlösung wovon? "Von dem Gesetz der Sünde und des Todes". Des Todes, welcher "der Sünde Sold" ist. Die frohe Botschaft Christi lautet: Gottes Strafe – die Todesstrafe – für die menschliche Übertretung des göttlichen Gebotes, vom Baume der Erkenntnis des Guten und Bösen zu essen und also gleich Gott werden zu wollen, ist aufgehoben. Auf welchem Wege? Auf dem Wege der Gnade. Dem Menschen ist seine Strafe gnadenweise erlassen, ja die Sünde vergeben. Es ist ihm sogar der Zugang zum Baum des Lebens und der Wiedereintritt ins Paradies Gottes verheißen. Die einzige Bedingung, an die der göttliche Akt der Gnade verknüpft ist, will der Mensch der Gnade teilhaftig werden, ist die, daß der Mensch die Gnade als Gnade (und nicht als sein "Recht") anerkennt, daß er seine Schuld und daß er eigentlich die Strafe durchaus verwirkt hat, bekennt und Buße tut: "Tut Buße, denn das Himmelreich ist nahe herbei gekommen," lautet daher wörtlich das Evangelium. Allerdings vermochte Gott das Urteil über den Menschen, der die Grenze zwischen Mensch und Gott hatte überschreiten wollen, nicht gleichsam bloß mit einem Federstrich aufzuheben. Es bedurfte wirklich eines Aktes, einer außerordentlichen Tat Gottes: von sich aus diese Grenze aufzuheben, indem er sie selber überschritt. In Christus hat Gott in der Tat die Sünde der Menschheit selber auf sich genommen: Daß der Mensch Gott hatte werden wollen, wird nunmehr durch Gottes Liebe damit vergolten, daß Gott selbst Mensch wird. Daß der Mensch gleichwie Gott und so frei vom Tode sein wollte, vergilt Gottes Liebe nun damit, daß Gott selbst in Menschengestalt den Tod auf sich nimmt. Gott erleidet den Tod, der Mensch erlangt das ewige Leben. Gott stirbt, der Mensch wird leben in Unsterblichkeit. Die Grenze zwischen Gott und Mensch ist (...) aufgehoben. Die alte Zwietracht zwischen Gott (und Göttern) und Menschen wird überwunden von Gottes Liebe, eines Gottes, der eben damit zum ersten Mal auch für die Menschen nicht mehr als eifersüchtiger (...), wenngleich gerechter Gott, als Gegenstand der Gottesfurcht erscheint, sondern liebenswürdig wird, und dies also dergestalt, daß göttliche Liebe zu den Menschen, menschliche Liebe Gottes und Liebe der Menschen zueinander in einer einzigen weltumfassenden Liebe zusammenfließen. Zwischen Gott und den Menschen herrschen

nunmehr Familienverhältnisse, in aller Form hergestellt durch eine Art Ehe zwischen Gott und Maria: Gott ist der Vater, Gottes Sohn ist auch ein Menschensohn, alle Menschen sind durch ihn Gottes Kinder.')
81. Jan Assmann, *The Price of monotheism* (Stanford, 2010), p. 67
82. Lars Gustafsson, *Gegen Null*, op. cit., p. 28 (in the German source: 'Den Sternenhimmel zu betrachten, bedeutet in die Vergangenheit zu sehen. Die meisten Sterne, die wir mit bloßem Auge erkennen, haben einen Abstand von mehr als 10 Lichtjahren. Die lokale Galaxie mit vielen hundert Milliarden Sternen hat einen Durchmesser von 100 000 Lichtjahren. Die nächste andere Galaxie, der Andromedanebel, ist 2 Millionen Lichtjahre entfernt. 50 Millionen Lichtjahre weit entfernt liegt eine Formation, zu der unser lokaler Teil gehört und die mehr als 500 000 Galaxien umfasst.')
83. Cf. *Midnight in Paris* by Woody Allen, released in 2011
84. Wisława Szymborska, "Our Ancestors' short lives", trans. Stanislaw Baranczak and Claire Cavanagh, in: *Poems, new and collected, 1957-1997* (New York, 1998), p. 194
85. Wisława Szymborska, "On Death, without exaggeration", trans. Stanislaw Baranczak and Claire Cavanagh, ibid., p. 189
86. Wisława Szymborska, "Written in a hotel", trans. Stanislaw Baranczak and Claire Cavanagh, ibid., pp. 91f.
87. Wisława Szymborska, "The Joy of writing", trans. Stanislaw Baranczak and Claire Cavanagh, ibid., p. 67
88. Wisława Szymborska, "Rehabilitation", trans. Stanislaw Baranczak and Claire Cavanagh, in: *Map: Collected and last poems* (New York, 2015), pp. 36f.
89. Wisława Szymborska, "In Praise of my sister", trans. Stanislaw Baranczak and Claire Cavanagh, ibid., p. 161
90. Ernst Tugendhat, *Anthropologie statt Metaphysik*, op. cit., p. 193
91. Jan Assmann, *The Price of monotheism*, op. cit., p. 90
92. As we can concur with Bernhard Waldenfels, every intercultural comparison is partial and plays out on the horizon of a given culture (cf. Bernhard Waldenfels, *Hyperphänomene – Modi leibhaftiger Erfahrung* ('Hyperphenomena – Modi of bodily experience') [Berlin, 2012], p. 338). Our own concepts are illuminated precisely in contrast with alien ideas. That is also how Jullien writes of his process: 'I confess, though, that I am more interested in the very conditions of my own particular thought and, to that end, in how (that is, by what strategy) I can gain some perspective within my own mind. For

this, the externality of Chinese thought, its deconstructive effect, is useful to me.' (François Jullien, *Vital nourishment – Departing from happiness* [Brooklyn, NY, 2007], p. 20)

93. François Jullien, *Du «temps»*. *Éléments d'une philosophie du vivre* (Paris, 2001). As no English translation exists at the date of this writing, translations are made instead from the German edition used by the author, i.e. *Über die »Zeit« - Elemente einer Philosophie des Lebens* (Zurich, 2010); here: p. 182 (in the German source: 'Der Ausdruck "Welchen Sinn hat das Leben?" offenbart die metaphysische Ebene unseres Denkens noch mitten in der geläufigen, alltäglichen Redeweise.')

94. Ibid. (in the German source: '(...) im klassischen Chinesisch findet man nichts, was dem nahe käme (sondern nur das "Schicksals-Los" des Lebens, *sheng-ming*); und ich wüßte auch kaum, wie man in modernes Chinesisch übersetzen könnte, welchen Sinn das Leben hat (es sei denn, ich propfe ihm eine neue Bedeutung auf; ich schwanke zwischen "Sinninhalt" (*yisi*)? oder welche "Wichtigkeit" (*yiyi*)? oder welchen "Wert" (*jiazhi*)? oder welches "Ziel" (*mudi*)?)')

95. Ibid., p. 34 (in the German source: 'mit unseren Begriffen gesagt, in einer Art "Infinitiv"')

96. Ibid., p. 108 (in the German source: 'man braucht ein *was* (*id*), das "sich präsentiert" und davor ist.')

97. Cf. Bernhard Waldenfels, *Bruchlinien der Erfahrung – Phänomenologie, Psychoanalyse, Phänomenotechnik* ('Faultlines of experience ... ') (Frankfurt, 2002)

98. François Jullien, *Über die »Zeit«*, op. cit., p. 88 (in the German source: 'sich Veränderndes')

99. Ibid., p. 22 (in the German source: 'in Korrelation befindlichen, polar konstituierten *Faktoren* (...)')

100. Ibid., p. 54 (in the German source: 'aber keiner weiß, wo')

101. The significance of the concept in orienting Western philosophy is demonstrated in the volume *Orientierung – Philosophische Perspektiven*, ed. W. Stegmaier (Frankfurt, 2005)

102. François Jullien, *Über die »Zeit«*, op. cit., pp. 74-75 (in the German source: 'integriert (...) auf globale Weise die unüberwindliche, ja unvorhersehbare Variabilität des Wetters, des *temps qu'il fait*, in jene Logik, die (im Wechsel) die Kontinuität der vergehenden Zeit, des *temps qui passe* erlaubt. Und dieser Verlauf ist durch die Jahreszeit hindurch keineswegs regelmäßig, sondern *reguliert* (...)')

103. Jullien describes the distinction between the concept *shi* and that of *momentum* as follows: '[*Shi*] is not the simple contraction of "movement" as conceived from a physical perspective and constituting a homogeneous time, the way our Latin etymology would have it (*momentum* comes from *movimentum*); rather, it carries in essence the marking of an occasion in and of itself (…).' Ibid., pp. 49–50 (in the German source: 'Er ist nicht die einfache Kontraktion der in physikalischer Perspektive aufgefaßten, eine homogene Zeit bildenden "Bewegung", wie es bei uns die lateinische Etymologie sagt (*momentum* kommt von *movimentum*), sondern er trägt wesentlich die Markierung einer Gelegenheit an sich (…).')

104. Ibid., p. 156 (in the German source: 'keineswegs sich mitreißen lassen; es bedarf einer inneren Strenge, weil sonst die Opportunität zum Opportunismus entartet. Das Problem ist also, das Folgen weder schwächlich noch passiv zu denken.')

105. Ibid., p. 170 (in the German source: 'wird erst durch seine Qualität wirklich spezifisch, und eben darin ist er der Jahreszeit verwandt')

106. Ibid., pp. 170–171 (in the German source: '(…) die am wenigsten "außerordentlichen" Momente können auch die tiefsten sein: sie "sammeln' am meisten (…): es kann dieser Moment sein, in dem wir gerade diese Worte wechseln, oder auch der Spaziergang, auf dem diese Worte gesprochen werden, oder auch, noch umfassender, der Aufenthalt am Meer, bei dem dieser Spaziergang stattfand…'); cf. also François Jullien, *Philosophy of living*, trans. M. Richardson (London, 2016), pp. 265ff.

107. François Jullien, Über die »Zeit«, op. cit., p. 186 (in the German source: 'Möglichkeit eines Zu-sich-kommen-Lassens (des Moments der Welt) von vornherein unterdrückt')

108. Ibid., p. 211 (in the German source: '(…) wo (…) "es nicht mehr geht", wenn der Lauf stockt, statt "fortzufahren", verzweifelt man und wird "sorgenvoll"…')

109. Ibid., p. 222 (in the German source: 'Weil der Tod nicht anders als das Leben natürlich ist, gibt es nichts Besonderes über ihn zu sagen.')

110. Thus Jullien writes that the expression 'trace' (*ji*) in Chinese usually describes the picture of an artist: 'In that first treatise on the art of painting, we have already moved from the "traces" manifested by the conduct and teaching of Confucius or Buddha, leading us to meditate on "that by which there is a trace", that is, the internal nature of wisdom, to the "traces" constituted by

painting' (François Jullien, *The Great Image Has No Form, or On the Nonobject through Painting'* [Chicago, 2009], p. 101)
111. Cf. François Jullien, *Detour and access: Strategies of meaning in China and Greece* (New York, 2000), p. 168: 'the Chinese tradition is wholly lacking in allegorical interpretation'.
112. Cf. ibid., p. 273 and p. 373
113. Cf. ibid., p. 308
114. François Jullien, *The Great image has no form*, op. cit., p. 219
115. François Jullien, *Detour and access*, op. cit., p. 236
116. On the question of the symbol in Ancient China, cf. ibid., p. 375
117. On the virtue of humanness according to Confucius, cf. ibid., p. 235
118. Lars Gustafsson, *Gegen Null*, op. cit., p. 30 (in the German source: 'Das überschaubare Universum, also das, was innerhalb des optischen Horizonts liegt, hat eine Tiefe von ungefähr 10 Milliarden Lichtjahren.')
119. Ibid., p. 28 (in the German source: '50 Millionen Lichtjahre weit entfernt liegt eine Formation, zu der unser lokaler Teil gehört und die mehr als 500 000 Galaxien umfasst.')
120. Jochen Rack, "Großvaters Tod" ('Grandfather's death'), in: *Lettre International*, No. 72 (Berlin, 2006), p. 92 (in the German original: '(...) *friedlich entschlafen*, wie man sagte, sah der Tote nicht aus, sondern von seinem Sterben wie nach einem Kampf grausam entstellt und verrenkt. Ich verstand, daß der Tod lange Zeit in der Geschichte der Menschheit als etwas gewaltsam von außen Zustoßendes erfahren wurde (...)')
121. Cited in Lars Gustafsson, *Gegen Null*, op. cit., p. 27; cf. Pascal, *Pensées*
122. Jan Assmann, *The Price of monotheism*, op. cit., p. 16
123. Cf. ibid., p. 24: 'Monotheism and polytheism are concepts born of the theological debates and controversies of the seventeenth and eighteenth centuries. As such, they are completely unsuitable for describing ancient religions. (...) God's oneness is not an invention of monotheism, but the central theme of polytheistic religions as well. This thesis (...) can be verified by examining any number of ancient Egyptian hymns.'
124. Ibid., p. 5
125. Jochen Rack, "Großvaters Tod", op. cit. (in the original German: 'In der medizinischen Terminologie war mein Großvater an Organversagen als Folge seines Krebsleidens gestorben, und der Arzt, den man nach seinem Tod gerufen hatte, kreuzte auf dem

Totenschein als Todesursache das Kästchen mit dem Begriff *'natürlich'* an.')
126. Jan Assmann, *The Price of monotheism*, op. cit., p. 44
127. Ludwig Wittgenstein, "Lectures on Religious Belief" from *Lectures and conversations on aesthetics, psychology and religious belief*, ed. Cyrul Barrett (Berkeley, 1967), p. 55
128. Ernst Tugendhat, *Anthropologie statt Metaphysik*, op. cit., p. 193 (in the original German: 'Es ist trivial, daß man die Existenz eines übernatürlichen Wesens ebensowenig widerlegen wie beweisen kann, aber das heißt eben nur, daß das einzige, was für sie spricht, der Wunsch ist, und damit ist dann zwar nicht die Existenz widerlegt, aber der Glaube an sie.')
129. Ibid., p. 192 (in the original German: 'Gott gibt es nicht, *und* das ist auch besser für uns (...).')
130. Ibid., p. 191 (in the original German: 'Ich glaube, daß einerseits das Bedürfnis nach einem Götterglauben nicht nur ein kulturelles, sondern ein anthropologisches, in der Struktur des menschlichen Seins begründetes Phänomen ist, daß es aber für einen heutigen Menschen, wenn er sich nichts vormacht, unmöglich ist, diesem Bedürfnis nachzugeben.')
131. Jan Assmann, *The Price of monotheism*, op. cit., p. 109
132. Cf. Paul Ricœur, *Living up to death*, op. cit., p. 69
133. Ibid., p. 63
134. Ibid., p. 71
135. Ibid., p. 85
136. Ibid., pp. 76f.
137. Ibid., p. 80
138. Ibid., p. 86. On the question of belief after Auschwitz, cf. Schalom Ben-Chorin, *Als Gott schwieg – Ein jüdisches Credo* ('When God was silent – a Jewish credo') (Mainz, 1989). This question comes to a head in Ben-Chorin's observation of a quotation from Elie Wiesel, who wrote in a personal confession: 'Never shall I forget that night, the first night in camp, that turned my life into one long night (...). Never shall I forget the small faces of the children whose bodies I saw transformed into smoke under a silent sky' ibid., pp. 87–88; and Ben-Chorin writes: 'There is no rejoinder to such an argument from the profundity of pain incurred,' ibid., p. 88 (in the original German: 'Gegen ein solches Argument aus der Tiefe des erlittenen Schmerzes gibt es keine Erwiderung.')
139. Paul Ricœur, *Living up to death*, op. cit., p. 16

140. Jorge Semprún, *L'Écriture ou la vie* (Paris, 1994), cited in Paul Ricœur, *Living up to death*, op. cit., p. 20
141. Jorge Semprún, *L'Écriture ou la vie* (Paris, 1994), cited in Paul Ricœur, *Living up to death*, op. cit., p. 25
142. Paul Ricœur, *Living up to death*, op.cit., p. 13. In this regard, Vladimir Jankélévitch is much more matter-of-fact: 'Man darf den Sterbenden nicht alleine lassen... Ohne Zweifel rührt die Vorstellung von der "Hilfe" im allgemeinen, auxilium, von der Sorge her, dem einsamen Menschen das Geleit zu geben und bei ihm zu sein. (...) Man kann dem einsam Sterbenden "Hilfe leisten", das heißt dem Sterbenden in der Stunde seines Todes beistehen, bis sein vorletzter Augenblick gekommen ist, doch kann man es ihm nicht abnehmen, den letzten Augenblick selbst und in eigener Person zu durchleben.' (Vladimir Jankélévitch, *Der Tod*, op. cit., pp. 38–39)
143. In his notes on the topic of resurrection, he only speaks of an 'intuition' and writes: 'From here to there: death reigns.' (Paul Ricœur, *Living up to death*, op. cit., p. 90)
144. Bernhard Waldenfels, *Schattenrisse der Moral* ('Silhouettes of morality') (Frankfurt, 2006), p. 106 (in the original German: *'Ich selbst beginne, aber nicht bei mir, sondern anderswo (...).'*)
145. François Jullien, Über die »Zeit«, op. cit., p. 19 (in the German source: '(...) um die Natur zu denken, muss der Physiker die Bewegung (*kinesis*) denken, die ihr Prinzip ist; und um die Bewegung zu denken, muß er, nach dem Ort, wo die Ortsveränderung stattfindet, die Zeit denken, die dazu dient, sie zu messen'.)
146. Published some years later in English as *The Crisis of European sciences and transcendental phenomenology*, trans. David Carr (Evanston, 1954)
147. Ingolf Dalferth, *Die Wirklichkeit des Möglichen – Hermeneutische Religionsphilosophie* (Tübingen, 2003), p. 531; cf. Bernhard Waldenfels, *Hyperphänomene*, op. cit., p. 389 (in the original German: 'Gott ist ganz anders, *als das, was hier von Gott gesagt oder dort über Gott gedacht wird*.')
148. Ibid. (in the original German: 'ist mit Motiven des Überschusses und des Entzugs vereinbar, während die totale Andersheit lediglich die Dialektik der Totalität ins Gegenteil verkehrt') Cf., for instance, Nietzsche's position in this case, as described above with a view to *The Antichrist*.

149. Ibid., p. 364 (in the original German: 'Wer dem Widerfahrnis vorweg Etwas oder Jemanden, einen Träger, einen Urheber oder auch einen Partner unterschiebt, überspringt die lebendige Erfahrung und fällt ihr ins Wort, bevor sie zur Sprache kommt. (...) Nehmen wir an, daß das Religiöse einer originären Erfahrung entspringt und kein bloß biologisches, psychologisches, politisches, ökonomisches oder imaginäres Epiphänomen darstellt. (...) Der Überschuß- und Fremdheitscharakter religiöser Widerfahrnisse ginge verloren, wollte man sie vorweg als religiös oder gottgegeben definieren. Strenggenommen gibt es also keine religiösen Phänomene oder religiösen Erfahrungen, es gibt nur ein Getroffensein und ein Angesprochensein, das sich in der Antwort des Religiösen, des Gläubigen als religiös, als göttlich erweist – oder eben nicht erweist. Die weitverbreiteten Projektionstheorien tun den zweiten Schritt vor dem ersten, indem sie das nachträgliche Als in das vorgängige Pathos zurückverlegen (...)')
150. The question of 'Whether' is posed, for instance, in view of the Taoist thought of an absolutely immanent, alternately regenerating and regulating homeostasis of what is naturally vital, as Jullien remarks (cf. François Jullien, *Vital nourishment*, op. cit., p. 140), without any difference – and question of meaning – to itself, as a sole generative and generous, continual kind of changing (cf. ibid., p. 77). In this thought, that also implies that 'the "other" in any of its guises is rigorously ignored' (ibid., p. 153; in this regard, cf. the responsive originating of the Other, the alien, in Waldenfels as well as thinking in terms of the alien in Jullien himself).
151. Regarding Levinas, cf. Emmanuel Levinas, *Totality and infinity – An Essay on exteriority* (The Hague, 1969), as well as his *Otherwise than being, or beyond essence* (The Hague, 1974)
152. Bernhard Waldenfels, *Hyperphänomene*, op. cit., p. 15 (in the original German: 'Eine Religionsphilosophie, die sich als Religionsphänomenologie versteht, ist weder religiös noch irreligiös. Sie kann nicht mehr tun, als Mißdeutungen abwehren und die Phänomene sprechen lassen, ohne das letzte Wort zu behalten.')
153. Bernhard Waldenfels, *Idiome des Denkens* ('Idioms of thinking') (Frankfurt, 2005), p. 36
154. François Jullien, Über die »Zeit«, op. cit., S. 200 (in the German source: '*fremd*, sondern "anrufend" (...)')
155. Bernhard Waldenfels, *Bruchlinien der Erfahrung – Phänomenologie, Psychoanalyse, Phänomenotechnik* ('Faultlines of experience ... '),

Frankfurt, 2002, p. 121 (in the original German: 'Daß Dinge uns (...) ansprechen, kann auch besagen, daß natürliche (...) Eigenkräfte freigesetzt werden, die über eine pragmatische und technische Nutzung der Dinge hinausgehen und teilhaben an dem, was uns ohne unser Zutun widerfährt. Diese vorgegenständlichen Erfahrungen sind zugleich der Nährboden für eine künstlerische, mythologisch-religiöse und denkende Gestaltung der Wirklichkeit, die den Rahmen der normalen Erfahrung übersteigt. Selbst die Askese wissenschaftlicher Forschung, die von der unmittelbaren Lebensbedeutsamkeit absieht, beläßt den Dingen ein Eigengewicht (...)')

156. We cannot feel that Nature has 'appealed' to us, according to Waldenfels, until a challenge addressed to us is associated with that appeal, that is, beyond the mere course of events representing much more an unaddressed experience we are faced with, one that befalls us anonymously. Nature 'does not mean us'; we think that 'we are meant' in our demand for an answer to the experience incurred. In this sense, with a view to that 'hostility' of Nature, Waldenfels would 'distinguish between destructive force that befalls us and annihilation that targets us' – that is, an unaddressed experience that we are faced with and an addressed *concern*; the destructive force of nature does not necessarily involve me, but it concerns me as an 'annihilation' of my Self, as an addressed threat (cf. ibid., pp. 109–113, on "Adressierte und unadressierte Aufforderungen" ('Addressed and unaddressed challenges'); the quote here is from a letter from Waldenfels to the author, dated 27 February 2013).

157. François Jullien, Über die »Zeit«, op. cit., p. 161 (in the German source: 'Nichts aber, das mehr im Übergang und dessen Natur schwerer zu entwirren wäre als das *Wasser*. In seiner feinsten Form ist es, bemerkt (...) (Wang Fuzhi), der kaum kondensierte, unerforschliche Niederschlag, der überall in der Atmosphäre verbreitet ist, und zugleich zeigt es sich in seiner umfassendsten Form in den Flußläufen und den Meeren, die sich nicht überqueren lassen. Es hat Anteil an beidem: an dem, was wie die Erde schon Form angenommen (...) hat, und an dem, was wie die Luft noch ganz in Bewegung ist.')

158. Bernhard Waldenfels, *Der Stachel des Fremden* ('The Sting of the alien') (Frankfurt, 1990), p. 93. We have to relate it above all not only to the human capability of conducting ourselves situationally but also to being able to speak of a situation as such, as well as of the mobility that has as a result opened up temporally and spatially. (cf.

Ernst Tugendhat, *Egocentricity and mysticism – An Anthropological study*, trans. A. Procyshyn and M. Wenning [New York, 2016], Chapter 1, "Propositional language and saying 'I' ")

159. Bernhard Waldenfels, *Der Stachel des Fremden*, op. cit.
160. Bernhard Waldenfels, *Sinnesschwellen – Studien zur Phänomenologie des Fremden 3* ('Sensory thresholds – Studies on the phenomenology of the alien 3') (Frankfurt, 1999), p. 91
161. Thus in this context Waldenfels remarks: 'Das exzessiv Unendliche, das uns vorschwebt [als Prozess der Differenzierung], setzt (...) voraus, daß das Unendliche weder in einem endlosen Werden noch in einem endgültigen Sein seinen Platz findet.' (Bernhard Waldenfels, *Hyperphänomene*, op. cit., p. 71) Doing so, he distances himself at the same time from Taoist notions of the world as endless change as well as from those ideas in the ontology of Antiquity and scholasticism and, as the case may be, in the fundamental ontology of Heidegger.
162. Cf. François Jullien, *Vital nourishment*, op. cit., p. 7
163. Cf. François Jullien, *Philosophy of living*, op. cit., pp. 265ff. Cf. in this regard also the bridge made to phenomenology, when Jullien recalls: 'I breathe *and* I perceive', thereby raising the question how a philosophy of breathing would relate to a phenomenology of perception, and vice versa (François Jullien, *The Great image has no form*, op. cit., p. 134).
164. Bernhard Waldenfels, *Bruchlinien der Erfahrung*, op. cit., p. 385 (in the original German: 'Problematisch wird die Funktionalisierung und Normalisierung, wenn der Überschuß des Ungleichen vergessen oder verdrängt wird. Das Nicht-Festgestelltsein des menschlichen Tieres würde auf diese Weise durch künstliche Feststellungen kompensiert.')
165. Bernhard Waldenfels, *Topographie des Fremden – Studien zur Phänomenologie des Fremden 1* ('Topography of the alien – Studies on the phenomenology of the alien 1') (Frankfurt, 1997), p. 156 (in the original German: 'Wie im Falle von Ich und Du handelt es sich um ein Kontrastphänomen, bei dem beide Kontrastwerte in eins entstehen. (...) Am Anfang steht *nicht eine Einheit, sondern eine Differenz.*')
166. Bernhard Waldenfels, *Idiome des Denkens*, op. cit., p. 107 (in the original German: 'Ich bin weder Urheber der Zeit, noch trifft die Zeit mich als etwas, was mir von außen zustößt; die geläufige Unterscheidung von Aktivität und Passivität versagt hier.')

167. Bernhard Waldenfels, *Ortsverschiebungen, Zeitverschiebunen – Modi leibhaftiger Erfahrung*, ('Shifts in place, shifts in time – *Modi* of bodily experience') (Frankfurt, 2009), p. 49 (in the original German: 'dem Überkreuz der Sehnerven gleicht (...)')
168. Bernhard Waldenfels, *Phänomenologie der Aufmerksamkeit* ('Phenomenology of attention') (Frankfurt, 2004), p. 167 (in the original German: 'daß er genötigt ist, Feststellungen zu treffen und sich selektiv auf ein bestimmtes Wie, auf ein So-und-nicht-anders festzulegen.')
169. Cf. Bernhard Waldenfels, *Antwortregister* ('Response register') (Frankfurt, 2007), p. 153
170. Bernhard Waldenfels, *Philosophisches Tagebuch – Aus der Werkstatt des Denkens, 1980-2005*, ('Philosophical diary ...'), ed. R. Guiliani (Munich, 2008), p. 99 (in the original German: 'Zu Blumenbergs *Arbeit am Mythos*, S. 27: Anthropogenese bedeutet Ablösung eines "eingespielten Anpassungssystems von Forderung und Leistung". Ich verstehe das so: Mensch als "nicht festgestelltes Tier". Diese *Unangepaßtheit* weist in zwei Richtungen: einerseits eine Wirklichkeit, die uns überrascht, überrumpelt, bedroht, unsere Wünsche und Entwürfe durchkreuzt – und andererseits unsere Aspirationen und Intentionen, die über die gegebene Wirklichkeit hinausdrängen: Potential an Wünschen und Phantasien. Doppelter Überschuß also, wie ein Arsenal von Fragen und Antworten, die sich nur zum Teil treffen – immer auch ein *Aneinandervorbeigehen* und -reden. Hier stellt sich die wichtige Frage, wie *Mangel* und Überschuß genau zu bestimmen und zu umgrenzen sind. Beides korrelativ ansetzen: die Wirklichkeit selber ist ambivalent.')
171. Thus Günter Eich wrote in his "Ode to Nature", 'We have our suspicions / on the subject of trout, winter, / and the speed of gravity.' (Günter Eich, *Angina days: Selected poems*, trans. Michael Hofmann [Princeton, 2010], p. 131)
172. In this context, Waldenfels writes: 'Mit Beginn der Neuzeit werden wir Zeuge einer *Radikalisierung des Möglichen*", und zwar derart, „daß die Ordnung selbst die Form eines Potentials annimmt. (...) Diese radikale Kontingenz bedeutet, daß Ordnung zugleich *ermöglicht* und *verunmöglicht*. (...) Das von ontologischen Schranken befreite und von moralischen Schranken nur notdürftig in Schach gehaltene Machenkönnen suggeriert Möglichkeiten einer endlosen Erweiterung des Spielraums. (...) Die Erweiterung der Spielräume durch Ausweitung der Verfügungsmacht, die Steigerung der Effekte

durch Prozeßbeschleunigung, die Vervielfältigung der Anschlüsse und die Entstehung von Netzwerken des Möglichen – all dies liegt auf der Hand. (...) Eine Alternative (...) würde nicht außerhalb der Machtentfaltung ansetzen, sondern in deren Mitte (...). In diesem Sinne zielen unsere Überlegungen auf eine Radikalisierung des Unmöglichen, die (...) aus der Erfahrung selbst erwächst' (Bernhard Waldenfels, *Hyperphänomene*, op. cit., pp. 84-87). In distinction to the 'contingency of actions' ('Handlungskontingenz') – along the lines of: *It could be different, too, and we can be different* – what is impossible for us ourselves would be constantly revealed in a contingency of events – in the sense of: *It could be different, too, but we cannot make it different* (cf. ibid., p. 269).
173. Cf. the following description by Jullien: 'Heaven, with its "steady" course and especially its diurnal and seasonal alternations, came to embody for the thinkers of Antiquity, and for Zhuangzi in particular,' the natural regulation of the great world process, which is consistent and thus constantly renews itself, engendering all that exists.' (François Jullien, *Vital nourishment*, op. cit., p. 43; see also p. 78, where in this respect he speaks of a 'homogeneous and continuous process'. See also Jullien's *Detour and access*, op. cit., p. 240, where we read that the 'the way of Heaven (the Tao) (...) because it never deviates (...) endlessly pursues its course and renews life.')
174. Cf. Ernst Tugendhat, *Egocentricity and mysticism*, op. cit.
175. Cf. Hans Belting, *An Anthropology of images: Picture, medium, body*, trans. Thomas Dunlap, Princeton, 2014, pp. 3ff.
176. Cf. Aristotle, *Poetics*, XXV, trans. S. H. Butcher (London, 1902), p. 97: 'The poet being an imitator, like a painter or any other artist, must of necessity imitate one of three objects – things as they were or are, things as they are said or thought to be, or things as they ought to be.'
177. Cf. the introduction of Oskar Bätschmann and Sandra Gianfreda to Leon Battista Alberti's treatise *On painting*: 'Das dritte Buch geht von Erfindung, Urteil und Auswahl des Malers aus und leitet diese in die Tätigkeiten der Hand in Skizze und Entwurf zur *istoria* über. Handtätigkeit und geistige Tätigkeit sind komplementär (...).' (Leon Battista Alberti, *Della Pittura – Über die Malkunst*, ed. O. Bätschmann and S. Gianfreda [Darmstadt, 2002], p. 28)
178. Maurice Merleau-Ponty, *Eye and mind*, trans. Michael Smith, in: *The Merleau-Ponty aesthetics reader* (Evanston, 1993), pp. 121-149, here: p. 125

NOTES 167

179. Ibid., p. 125
180. Ibid., p. 129
181. Cf. Hans-Jörg Rheinberger, *Epistemology of the concrete* (Durham, NC, 2010)
182. This reference could readily be compared with Bernhard Waldenfels' observations on phenomenotechniques in his book *Bruchlinien der Erfahrung* ('Faultlines of experience') from 2002.
183. The verse comes from her poem "Sky", contained in the volume: Wisława Szymborska, *Poems, new and collected*, op. cit., p. 224
184. Maurice Merleau-Ponty, *The Visible and the invisible*, op. cit., pp. 84f.
185. Bernhard Waldenfels, *In den Netzen der Lebenswelt* ('In the nets of the lifeworld') (Frankfurt, 2005), p. 16 (in the original German: 'Ablösung und Verselbständigung wissenschaftlicher Konstruktionen'). On the topic of bottomlessness, see my essay "Dreams of the sighted in the polar night", in: Geert Goiris, *Whiteout* (Leuven, 2011)
186. Ludger Schwarte, *Philosophie der Architektur* ('Philosophy of architecture') (Munich, 2009), p. 16 (in the original German: 'nicht länger auf einem Ursprungs-Mythos [...] sondern auf wechselseitigen Begründungszusammenhängen')
187. Cf. Bernhard Waldenfels, *In den Netzen der Lebenswelt*, op. cit., p. 37
188. Jullien elaborates in the following quote from the German version of his text: '(...) was die Philosophie nicht gedacht hat – was sie angefangen hat fallen zu lassen, was sie fallen lassen *mußte* –, ist das, was man nur allzugut »weiß«, weil es zu vertraut ist (»tief Atem holen«,»nimm dir Zeit, Atem zu holen«...), das aber eben darum nicht distanziert und distinkt genug ist, um sich als Denk-*Objekt* zu konstituieren, und infolgedessen kein theoretisches Interesse auf sich hat ziehen können. Und wenn ich hier von einer impliziten, verdeckten Wahl, mit anderen Worten von Voreingenommenheit spreche, dann weil so viele Philosophen, die *alle*, einschließlich der Phänomenologie (in Frankreich von Descartes bis Merleau-Ponty), von einer »Philosophie der Wahrnehmung« ausgegangen sind [author's note: this statement could be much more nuanced], sich einander abgelöst, sich kritisiert, sich gespalten, kurz, immer wieder einen neuen Aufbruch versucht haben, ohne jemals daran zu denken (...), was eine, sich als ein anderer Ausgangspunkt der Philosophie konstituierende, *Philosophie der Atmung* wäre.' (François Jullien, *Über die »Zeit«*, op. cit., pp. 193-194)

189. Cf. Maurice Merleau-Ponty, *Eye and mind*, op. cit., p. 129
190. Paul Ricœur, *Living up to death*, op. cit., p. 8
191. From the poem "May 16, 1973", transl. Stanislaw Baranczak and Claire Cavanagh, in: Wisława Szymborska, *Poems, new and collected*, op. cit., p. 246
192. In the poem "Soliloquy for Cassandra", transl. Stanislaw Baranczak and Claire Cavanagh, in: Wisława Szymborska, *Poems, new and collected*, op. cit., pp. 83f., here: p. 84
193. Ibid., pp. 252f.
194. Ernst Tugendhat, *Anthropologie statt Metaphysik*, op. cit., p. 165 (in the original German: 'Erst wenn man die Angst vor dem Tod als Kehrseite des Willens weiterzuleben sieht, wird verständlich, warum man diese Angst nicht aus der Ferne empfindet. Der Wille weiterzuleben ist immer auf das nächste Lebensstück bezogen, er ist nicht ein darüber schwebender Wille zum Leben als solchem (...).')
195. Ernst Tugendhat, *Über den Tod* ('On Death') (Frankfurt, 2006), p. 16 (in the original German: 'daß wir irgendeinmal sterben werden bzw. daß wir jederzeit sterben können (...)')
196. Paul Ricœur, *Living up to death*, op. cit., pp. 27f.
197. Ernst Tugendhat, *Über den Tod*, op. cit., p. 52 (in the original German: 'So gesehen, legt der Tod auf die Frage, vor die er stellt, selbst eine Antwort nahe, aber es ist nicht leicht, sie zu ergreifen.')
198. The picture is called *Le sourire* ('The smile'), and comes from his 'sunny' Surrealist period. It was created in 1943 and is found today in the collection of the Royal Museums for Fine Arts in Brussels, in the exhibition hall of the Magritte Museum there. The tombstone displayed bears the inscription 'An[no] 192370'.
199. Jullien notes in this regard: 'By conceiving of the ideal of "availability" as a *comprehensive* disposition of his personality, so that he was equally open to any and every possibility and did not rule anything out *a priori*, his conduct "evolved" solely in response to his situation. He therefore ultimately fails to develop any *position* vis-à-vis power – for a position implies an end to flow, blockage, and partiality. By refusing to take sides, "standing neither for nor against," as Confucius recommended, he has made it impossible for himself to constitute *another side* (different from that of power) and closed off the possibility of dissidence. Thus the Chinese man of letters never transformed himself into an intellectual, backed by an order of values other than that derived from history. For a – liberating – order of the political to have been constituted and institutionalized,

an ideal would have had to be designated, an ideal distinct from the functionality of process, which Chinese thought conceptualized as permanently harmonious. In other words, a utopia would have to have been produced.' In addition it was traditionally assumed that the 'state apparatus (...) was supposed to maintain the great natural regulation at the human level'. (François Jullien, *Vital nourishment*, op. cit., pp. 154-156)
200. Cf. Hannah Arendt, *The Human condition*, second edition (Chicago, 1998)
201. In the poem "A Tale begun," trans. Stanislaw Baranczak and Claire Cavanagh, in: Wisława Szymborska, *Poems, new and collected*, p. 210
202. Hannah Arendt, *The Human condition*, op. cit., p. 246
203. Cf. the following observation of Byung-Chul Han in the original German source: 'Im friedlichen, freundlichen Mitsein mit den Dingen, bekommt man auch Augen für den Anderen. Der lange Blick, vor dem Dinge und Natur sich ausbreiten, sich in ihrem So-Sein ausruhen, ist auch der Freundlichkeit gegenüber dem Anderen (autrui) eingeschrieben.' (Byung-Chul Han, *Tod und Alterität* ['Death and alterity'] [Munich, 2002], p. 132)
204. François Jullien, Über die »Zeit«, op. cit., p. 201 (in the German source: 'in der gelebt wird')
205. Byung-Chul Han, *Tod und Alterität*, op. cit., p. 225 (in the original German: 'Die Endlichkeit (...) ermöglicht (...) eine singuläre Erfahrung der Zeit als Gabe.')
206. Cf. Lieh-Tzü [Liezi], *Taoist teachings from the book of Lieh-Tzü*, transl. Lionel Giles (London, 1912), pp. 102f.; also cited in Byung-Chul Han, *Tod und Alterität*, op. cit., p. 214 (in the original German, excerpted by Han from Liä-Dsi, *Das wahre Buch vom quellenden Urgrund*: 'Unter den Leuten von We lebte ein Mann namens Wu vom Osttor. Als sein Sohn starb, ward er nicht traurig. Da sprach sein Hausverwalter zu ihm: »Auf der ganzen Welt gab es keinen Menschen, der seinen Sohn so liebte wie Ihr. Nun Euer Sohn gestorben ist, warum seid Ihr nicht traurig?« Wu vom Osttor sprach: »Es gab eine Zeit, da ich immer ohne Sohn war, und in jener Zeit, da ich noch keinen Sohn hatte, war ich nicht traurig. Nun ist mein Sohn gestorben, und es ist wieder ebenso wie früher, da ich noch keinen Sohn hatte. Was sollte ich da traurig sein?« ')
207. Cf. François Jullien, Über die »Zeit«, op. cit., p. 182
208. According to the corpus of the *Zhuangzi*, Jullien says, the author justifies himself 'on thoroughly naturalist grounds – not having to

mourn the death of his wife' (François Jullien, *Vital nourishment*, op. cit., p. 69)
209. Emmanuel Levinas, "Language and proximity," in: *Collected philosophical papers*, trans. A. Lingis (Dordrecht, 1987), pp. 109-126, here: p. 118
210. Luce Irigaray, *An Ethics of sexual difference*, trans. C. Burke and G. Gill (London, 2005), p. 175
211. Emmanuel Levinas, "Language and proximity", op. cit., p. 119
212. Paul Ricœur, *Living up to death*, op. cit., p. 12
213. Ernst Tugendhat, *Anthropologie statt Metaphysik*, op. cit., p. 165 (in the original German: 'Erst wenn man die Angst vor dem Tod als Kehrseite des Willens weiterzuleben sieht, wird verständlich, warum man diese Angst nicht aus der Ferne empfindet. Der Wille weiterzuleben ist immer auf das nächste Lebensstück bezogen, er ist nicht ein darüber schwebender Wille zum Leben als solchem, und deswegen ist auch die Angst vor dem Tod auf das jeweils nächste Lebensstück gerichtet.'); cf. fn. 194 above.
214. Ernst Tugendhat, *Über den Tod*, op. cit., p. 55 (in the original German: 'Man könnte die Gelassenheit vielleicht ihrerseits unter den Realitätssinn subsumieren, weil sie sich besonders dann nahelegt, wenn das Festhalten als irrational erscheint, ähnlich wie wir ein Übermaß an Emotionen zu vermeiden versuchen, wo wir dieses als realitätsunangemessen erkennen, ohne deswegen die Emotionalität als solche zu verachten. Das führt schließlich zur Frage nach der anzustrebenden Ausgewogenheit zwischen Festhalten und Kämpfen einerseits und Loslassen andererseits. Denn um Ausgewogenheit scheint es sich doch handeln zu müssen. Die schlichte Lebensverneinung, wie der Buddha sie lehrte, wirkt ebenso fragwürdig wie die sture Selbstbehauptung. Das Loslassen, die Gelassenheit, ist im übrigen eine Haltung, die wir uns nicht nur dem Tod gegenüber wünschen, sondern in allem unseren Tun und Trachten (...).')
215. Ibid., pp. 57-58 (in the original German: 'vor denen wir uns gestellt sehen (...): Fragen, wie wir leben wollen, nicht Fragen, wie wir sind (...)')
216. The film was directed by James Mangold and released in theatres in 2005.
217. He writes: 'Sie starb ruhig, ohne Schmerzen. Ihre große Familie war um sie versammelt. Kein Kampf, sie willigte wohl in den Abschied (...). Wenn wir hier um sie trauern, so mit Dankbarkeit,

in schmerzlicher Freude, in unserer Freiheit.' (Volker Braun, "Ein Schutzengelgeschwader", in: *Die Zeit*, No. 51 [Hamburg, 15 December 2011], p. 56)

218. Astrid Lindgren added this episode into the TV series, adapted from the chapter "Pippi arranges a picnic" from her book *Pippi Longstocking*; cf. Astrid Lindgren, *Pippi Longstocking* (New York, 1950), in addition to Astrid Lindgren. *Pippi Longstocking* (teleplay), Episode 4: "Pippi arranges a picnic" (U.S. release 1973)

219. In view of this deeply disconcerting awareness, I believe Jankélévitch has found a very poignant term of expression: 'Der zum Tod seines eigenen Lebens konvertierte Lebende (...).' (Vladimir Jankélévitch, *Der Tod*, op. cit., p. 78) The awareness of our own limits asks for a way to relate to them, in life. As a result of their intangibility, they become no object of knowledge. At the same time, the experience of this intangibility is perceptible. In this case there is a predisposition for what is apparent yet not tangible, not as something. It is the singular experience of the alien, as that which eludes what is our own, puts challenges *to what is our own*, as Waldenfels describes in xenology, his responsive phenomenology and doctrine of the alien. The intensity of the experience of our own limits effects a fund which demands its own way of dealing with it, in whatever form that may be. It corresponds to a radical turning point in thinking, in the way we take a stance in life. That is why I consider Jankélévitch's formulation to the point in this instance.

220. *Deshalb leben wir* (Frankfurt, 1980) is the German translation of Wisława Szymborska's first collection of poetry, published in Poland as *Dlatego żyjemy* ('Why we live', 1952)

221. In the poem "The Joy of writing", transl. Stanislaw Baranczak and Claire Cavanagh, in: *Poems, new and collected, 1957-1997* (New York, 1998), p. 67

222. In the poem "Written in a hotel", ibid., pp. 91f.

223. In the poem "A Tale begun", ibid., p. 210

224. In: *Nobel lectures: From the literature laureates, 1986 to 2006* (New York, 2007), pp. 144-149

225. In the poem "Life while-you-wait", trans. by Clare Cavanagh and Stanislaw Baranczak, in: Wisława Szymborska, *Map: Collected and last poems* (New York, 2015), pp. 228f.

226. Jankélévitch writes, for instance: 'Geliebt haben, und mehr nicht.' (Vladimir Jankélévitch, *Der Tod*, op. cit., p. 560) Love as exposé is, of course, a traditionally Western theme, as Jullien notes (cf.

François Jullien, *The Great image has no form*, op. cit., p. 21; as well as his *Vital nourishment*, op. cit., pp. 126f. and p. 61: 'Chinese thinkers conceived of love solely as emotion, or as playing a sexual role in cosmic regulation.'). In 1931, the Japanese writer Tanizaki Jun'ichirō wrote: 'Die Tendenz, Liebe (...) abzuwerten, (...) ist in Ostasien allgemein keineswegs ungewöhnlich. (...) Es mangelt (...) nicht an Werken, die die Liebe behandeln. Aber sie haben in unserer Literaturgeschichte erst von dem Zeitpunkt an Beachtung gefunden, als die westliche Betrachtungsweise sich auszubreiten begann.' (Tanizaki Jun'ichirō, *Liebe und Sinnlichkeit* [Zurich, 2011], p. 10). He continues: 'Zwar wäre es nicht richtig, zu behaupten, dass in unserer Tradition eine Kunst, die die Liebe thematisiert, überhaupt nicht anerkannt wurde – tatsächlich bewunderte man sie im Stillen sehr und delektierte sich mit großem Vergnügen daran -, nach außen aber tat man möglichst so, als wisse man von nichts. Das war unsere Art der Zurückhaltung – eine auf stillschweigende Übereinkunft basierende gesellschaftliche Etikette.' (Ibid., p. 16) (For the English translation, cf. Tanizaki Jun'ichirō, "Love and sexual desire", trans. Thomas LaMarre, in: *Shadows on the screen* [Ann Arbor, 2005], pp. 319-355) The East Asian preference for friendliness – as repeatedly described by Byung Chul-Han in his writings – and the Western accentuation of love is seen by the author François Cheng – born in Nanjing in 1929 and living in Paris since 1949 – in a relationship that presents a special challenge today, in light of globalisation: 'L'Occident a surtout chanté la passion amoureuse, les lettrés chinois ont porté l'amitié à un degré absolu. Il me semble devenir essentiel, à notre époque, de réfléchir sur les liens et les contradictions de l'amour et l'amitié, sur la manière dont les deux peuvent se nourrir et peut-être se rehausser.' (*Le Monde*, Paris, 25 May 2012, 'Le Monde des livres' supplement, p. 12)

227. In the poem "Nothing nothinged itself for me as well", in: Wisława Szymborska, *Miracle fair: Selected poems of Wisława Szymborska*, trans. Joanna Trzeciak (New York, 2001), p. 113

List of illustrations

Ill. 1. Master of the *Thennsche Kinderbildnisse* ('Likenesses of the Thenn Children'), *Three Children of Johann Thenn, Master of the Mint*: *Likeness of Ruprecht Thenn*, lime tree wood, 43 × 34 cm; *Likeness of Wolf (?) Thenn*, lime tree wood, 46.80 × 36.20 cm; *Likeness of Barbara Thenn*, lime tree wood, 43.20 × 34.20 cm; Frankfurt, Städel Museum, photo by U. Edelmann

Ill. 2. Master of the *Thennsche Kinderbildnisse*, *Likeness of Ruprecht Thenn*, lime tree wood, 43 × 34 cm, Frankfurt, Städel Museum, photo by U. Edelmann

Ill. 3. Jan Gossaert, *The Children of Christian II, King of Denmark*, oil on oak panel, 34 × 46 cm, 1526, London, Collection of Her Majesty the Queen of England by permission of the Royal Collection Trust / © Her Majesty Queen Elizabeth II 2017

Ill. 4. Joshua Reynolds, *Lesbia*, oil on canvas, undated, 75 × 67.20 cm, London, Tate Gallery

Ill. 5. Joshua Reynolds, *Girl with a Dead Bird*, oil on canvas, undated, 73.70 × 61 cm, private collection (cat. no. 2083)

Ill. 6. Joshua Reynolds, *Girl with a Dead Bird*, oil on canvas, undated, 76.20 × 63.50 cm, private collection (cat. no. 2084)

Ill. 7. Jean-Baptiste Greuze, *A Girl with a Dead Canary*, oil on canvas, 1765, 53.30 × 46.00 cm, NG 435, National Galleries of Scotland, bequest of Lady Murray of Henderland 1861

Bibliography

Adorno, Theodor W., *Aesthetic theory*, trans. Robert Hullot-Kentor (London, 1997)
Leon Battista Alberti, *Della Pittura – Über die Malkunst*, ed. O. Bätschmann and S. Gianfreda (Darmstadt, 2002)
Alte Meister – 1300-1800 im Städel Museum, exhibition catalogue (Frankfurt; Ostfildern, 2011)
Arendt, Hannah, *The Human condition*, second edition (Chicago, 1998)
Aristotle, *Poetics*, trans. S. H. Butcher (London, 1902)
Assmann, Jan, *The Price of monotheism* (Stanford, 2010)
Barker, Emma, *Greuze and the painting of sentiment* (Cambridge, 2005)
Bedaux, Jan Baptist, and Rudi Ekkart, eds, *Kinderen op hun mooist. Het kinderportret in de Nederlanden 1500-1700*, exhibition catalogue, Museum of Fine Arts, Antwerp, Frans Hals Museum, Haarlem; Engl. trans. *Pride and joy. Children's portraits in the Netherlands 1500-1700* (Ghent; Amsterdam, 2000)
Belting, Hans, *An Anthropology of images: Picture, medium, body* (Princeton, 2011)
---, *The End of the history of art?* (Chicago, 1987)
Ben-Chorin, Schalom, *Als Gott schwieg – Ein jüdisches Credo* (Mainz, 1989)
Berger, Renate, *Rodolfo Valentino – Biografie* (Hamburg, 2003)
Blumenberg, Hans, *Ästhetische und metaphorologische Schriften* (Frankfurt, 2001)
---, *Lebenszeit und Weltzeit* (Frankfurt, 2001)
Boehm, Rudolf, *Grundriß einer Poietik* (Würzburg, 2005)
---, *Kritik der Grundlagen des Zeitalters* (The Hague, 1974)
Braun, Volker, "Ein Schutzengelgeschwader", in: *Die Zeit*, No. 51 (Hamburg, 15 December 2011), p. 56
Busch, Werner, *Great wits jump – Laurence Sterne und die bildende Kunst* (Munich, 2011)
Claessens, Bob, "Fillette à l'oiseau mort", in: *Peinture vivante*, 6, Cultura ed. (Brussels, 1968-1969)
Dalferth, Ingolf, *Die Wirklichkeit des Möglichen – Hermeneutische Religionsphilosophie* (Tübingen, 2003)
Das große deutsche Märchenbuch, ed. H. Brackert (Munich, Zurich; 1994)
De brieven van Rubens, ed. L. Huet (Amsterdam, 2006)

176 BIBLIOGRAPHY

De Firma Brueghel, ed. Peter v. d. Brink (Ghent; Amsterdam, 2002)
Diderot, Denis, *Diderot on Art*, Vols. *I and II*, trans. John Goodman (New Haven, 1995)
Diogenes Laertius, *Lives and opinions of eminent philosophers*, trans. R. D. Hicks (Cambridge, MA, 1925)
Ecker, Jürgen, *Anselm Feuerbach. Leben und Werk, Kritischer Katalog der Gemälde, Ölskizzen und Ölstudien*, catalogue raisonné (Munich, 1991)
Eich, Günter, *Angina days: Selected poems*, trans. Michael Hofmann (Princeton, 2010)
Eichberger, Dagmar, *Leben mit Kunst, Wirken durch Kunst – Sammelwesen und Hofkunst unter Margarete von Österreich, Regentin der Niederlande* (Turnhout, 2002)
L'Empire interdit – Visions du monde des maîtres chinois et flamands, exhibition catalogue (Brussels, 2007)
Forest, Philippe, *Tous les enfants sauf un* (Paris, 2007)
Theodor Gomperz, *Greek thinkers: A History of ancient philosophy*, 3 vols., trans. L. Magnus and G. Berry (New York, 1905)
Grimm, Jacob and Wilhelm, "The Companionship of cat and mouse", in: *The Original folk and fairy tales of the Brothers Grimm*, trans. and ed. Jack Zipes, reprint (Princeton, 2016)
Grimm, Jacob and Wilhelm, "Katze und Maus in Gesellschaft", in: *Das große deutsche Märchenbuch*, ed. H. Brackert (Munich; Zurich, 1994)
Gustafsson, Lars, *Gegen Null – Eine mathematische Phantasie* (Zurich, 2011)
Han, Byung-Chul, *Abwesen – Zur Kultur und Philosophie des Fernen Ostens* (Berlin, 2007)
---, *Philosophie des Zen-Buddhismus* (Stuttgart, 2002)
---, *Tod und Alterität* (Munich, 2002)
---, *Todesarten – Philosophische Untersuchungen zum Tod* (Munich, 1998)
Hartung, Harald, *Der Tag vor dem Abend – Aufzeichnungen* (Göttingen, 2012)
Heine, Heinrich, *The Harz journey and selected prose*, trans. R. Robertson (London, 1993)
Husserl, Edmund, *Die Krisis der europäischen Wissenschaften und die transzendentale Phänomenologie* ([Freiburg,] 1936); English trans. *The Crisis of European sciences and transcendental phenomenology*, trans. David Carr (Evanston, 1954)
Imdahl, Max, *Giotto – Arenafresken. Ikonographie, Ikonologie, Ikonik* (Munich, 1996)
Irigaray, Luce, *An Ethics of sexual difference*, trans. C. Burke and G. Gill (London, 2005)

Jankélévitch, Vladimir, *Der Tod* (Frankfurt, 2005)
De Jongh, Eddy, "Erotica in vogelperspectief – De dubbelzinnigheid van een reeks 17de eeuwse genrevoorstellingen", in: *Simiolus, Kunsthistorisch tijdschrift*, Vol. 3 (1968-69), pp. 48-49
Jullien, François, *Detour and access: Strategies of meaning in China and Greece*, trans. Sophie Hawkes (New York, 2000)
---, *Du « temps ». Éléments d'une philosophie du vivre* (Paris, 2001); German trans. *Über die »Zeit« – Elemente einer Philosophie des Lebens* (Zurich, 2010)
---, *The Great Image Has No Form, or On the Nonobject through Painting*, trans. Jane Marie Todd (Chicago, 2009)
---, *Philosophy of living*, trans. Michael Richardson (London, 2016)
---, *The Silent transformations*, trans. Krysztof Fijalkowski and Michael Richardson (London; New York, 2011)
---, *Vital nourishment – Departing from happiness*, trans. Arthur Goldhammer (Brooklyn, NY, 2007)
Jun'ichirō, Tanizaki, *Liebe und Sinnlichkeit* (Zurich, 2011); English trans. "Love and sexual desire", trans. Thomas LaMarre, in: *Shadows on the screen* (Ann Arbor, 2005), pp. 319-355
Kierkegaard, Søren, *The Concept of anxiety*, ed. and trans. Reidar Thomte (Princeton, 1980)
Korteweg, Anton, "With a Poet's Eye – A Few Dutch Poems on Dutch Paintings", in: *The Low Countries – Arts and Society in Flanders and the Netherlands*, RNS 1103, No. 19 (Rekkem; Raamsdonksveer, 2011)
Lessing, Gotthold Ephraim, *Laocoön: An Essay on the limits of painting and poetry*, trans. E. A. McCormick (Baltimore, 1984)
Levi, Primo, "In the park", in: *A Tranquil star: Unpublished stories of Primo Levi*, trans. and ed. Ann Goldstein and Alessandra Bastagli (New York, 2007)
Levinas, Emmanuel, "Language and proximity," in: *Collected philosophical papers*, trans. Alphonso Lingis (Dordrecht, 1987), pp. 109-126
---, *Otherwise than being, or beyond essence*, trans. Alphonso Lingis (The Hague, 1974)
---, *Time and the other*, trans. Richard A. Cohen (Pittsburgh, 1987)
---, *Totality and infinity – An Essay on exteriority*, trans. Alphonso Lingis (The Hague, 1969)
Lieh-Tzü [Liezi], *Taoist teachings from the book of Lieh-Tzü*, transl. Lionel Giles (London, 1912)
Lindgren, Astrid, *Pippi Longstocking* (New York, 1950)
Mannings, David, *Sir Joshua Reynolds – A Complete catalogue of his paintings* (New Haven; London, 2000).

Martin, Charles, *Catullus* (New Haven, 1992)
Merleau-Ponty, Maurice, *Eye and mind*, trans. Michael Smith, in: *The Merleau-Ponty aesthetics reader* (Evanston, 1993), pp. 121-149
---, *The Visible and the invisible*, ed. C. Lefort, trans. Alphonso Lingis (Evanston, 1968)
Mühleis, Volkmar, "Dreams of the sighted in the polar night", in: Goiris, Geert, *Whiteout* (Leuven, 2011)
Nietzsche, Friedrich, *The Antichrist*, trans. Walter Kaufmann, in: *The Portable Nietzsche*, ed. Walter Kaufmann (New York, 1976)
Nobel lectures: From the literature laureates, 1986 to 2006 (New York, 2007)
Orientierung – Philosophische Perspektiven, ed. W. Stegmaier (Frankfurt, 2005)
Ovid, *Metamorphoses*, trans. Charles Martin (New York, 2004)
Panofsky, Erwin, *Aufsätze zu Grundfragen der Kunstwissenschaft* (Berlin, 1985)
---, *Meaning in the Visual Arts* (New York, 1955)
Philosophisches Wörterbuch, ed. Georgi Schischkoff (Stuttgart, 1991)
Rack, Jochen, "Großvaters Tod", in: *Lettre International*, No. 72 (Berlin, 2006)
Rheinberger, Hans-Jörg, *Epistemology of the concrete* (Durham, NC, 2010)
Ricœur, Paul, *Living up to death*, trans. David Pellauer (Chicago, 2009)
---, *Memory, history, forgetting*, trans. Kathleen Blamey and David Pellauer (Chicago, 2004)
De Rynck, Patrick, *Dit is België – In tachtig meesterwerken* (Amsterdam, 2010)
Sandvoss, Ernst R., *Geschichte der Philosophie* (Munich, 1989)
Schwarte, Ludger, *Philosophie der Architektur* (Munich, 2009)
Semprún, Jorge, *L'Écriture ou la vie* (Paris, 1994)
Shawe-Taylor, D., and J. Scott, *Brueghel to Rubens – Masters of Flemish Painting* (London, 2007)
Stoichita, Victor I., *The Self-Aware Image. An Insight Into Early Modern Meta-Painting* (Turnhout, 2015)
Szymborska, Wisława, *Deshalb leben wir*, trans. and ed. Karl Dedecius (Frankfurt, 1980)
---, *Die Gedichte*, trans. and ed. Karl Dedecius (Frankfurt, 1997)
---, *Map: Collected and last poems*, trans. Stanislaw Baranczak and Claire Cavanagh (New York, 2015)
---, *Miracle fair: Selected poems of Wisława Szymborska*, trans. Joanna Trzeciak (New York, 2001)
---, *Poems, new and collected, 1957-1997*, trans. Stanislaw Baranczak and Claire Cavanagh (New York, 1998)

Toorians, Lauran, "Portrait of the Child as Sitter – *Children of a Golden Age*", in: *The Low Countries – Arts and Society in Flanders and the Netherlands*, Stichting Ons Erfdeel (Rekkem; Raamsdonksveer, 2001)
Tugendhat, Ernst, *Anthropologie statt Metaphysik* (Munich, 2010)
---, *Egocentricity and mysticism – An Anthropological study*, trans. A. Procyshyn and M. Wenning (New York, 2016)
---, *Über den Tod* (Frankfurt, 2006)
Van der Stighelen, Katlijne, *Hoofd en bijzaak. Portretkunst in Vlaanderen van 1420 tot nu* (Leuven, 2008)
Van Puyvelde, Leo, "L'application de la radiographie aux tableaux", in: *Journal de radiologie et d'électrologie*, Paris, Vol. XVII, No. 2 (February, 1933)
---, "L'enfant à l'oiseau mort – Un portrait de Marguerite d'Autriche par Juan de Flandres", in: *Les Arts Plastiques*, No. 7-8 (Brussels, 1948)
Waldenfels, Bernhard, *Antwortregister* (Frankfurt, 2007)
---, *Bruchlinien der Erfahrung – Phänomenologie, Psychoanalyse, Phänomenotechnik* (Frankfurt, 2002)
---, *Hyperphänomene – Modi hyperbolischer Erfahrung* (Berlin, 2012)
---, *Idiome des Denkens* (Frankfurt, 2005)
---, *In den Netzen der Lebenswelt* (Frankfurt, 2005)
---, *Ortsverschiebungen, Zeitverschiebungen – Modi leibhaftiger Erfahrung*, (Frankfurt, 2009)
---, *Phänomenologie der Aufmerksamkeit* (Frankfurt, 2004)
---, *Phenomenology of the Alien: Basic Concepts*, trans. Tanja Stähler and Alexander Kozin (Evanston, 2011)
---, *Philosophisches Tagebuch – Aus der Werkstatt des Denkens, 1980-2005*, ed. R. Guiliani (Munich, 2008)
---, *Schattenrisse der Moral* (Frankfurt, 2006)
---, *Sinnesschwellen – Studien zur Phänomenologie des Fremden 3* (Frankfurt, 1999)
---, *Topographie des Fremden – Studien zur Phänomenologie des Fremden 1* (Frankfurt, 1997)
---, *Der Stachel des Fremden* (Frankfurt, 1990)
Weniger, Matthias, *Sittow, Morros, Juan de Flandes – Drei Maler aus dem Norden am Hof Isabellas der Katholischen* (Kiel, 2011)
Wittgenstein, Ludwig, *Lectures and conversations on aesthetics, psychology and religious belief*, ed. Cyrul Barrett (Berkeley, 1967)
Wölfflin, Heinrich, *Principles of art history. The Problem of the development of style in later art* (New York, 1932)
Women of Distinction. Margaret of York / Margaret of Austria, exhibition catalogue Mechelen Lamot, ed. D. Eichberger (Leuven, 2005)

www.ingramcontent.com/pod-product-compliance
Lightning Source LLC
Chambersburg PA
CBHW031627210526
45464CB00004B/1791